DISCIPLE OF LIBERTY

SEVEN PRIORITIES OF A CHRISTIAN PATRIOT

JASON RINK

Published by:

The Liberty Voice, LLC

ISBN: 978-0-9827180-0-1

The Liberty Voice, LLC

To contact the publisher or the author:

www.thelibertyvoice.com

www.jasonrink.com

Special thanks to:

Cover Design: Terry Ladrach, Rebel's Cry Multimedia

Front Cover Photographs: Remington Phillips

Back Cover Photograph: Geoffrey Shough

Editors: Tisa Rink and James Rink

This book is dedicated to my wife Tisa, whose friendship and encouragement kept me going, and to my son, Ethan, the other writer in the family.

Contents

Introduction: Christians at a
Crossroads..................................1

Chapter One: Define the Limits of
Authority................................15

Chapter Two: Demand Fidelity to the
Constitution.............................29

Chapter Three: Defend Liberty for All
People....................................43

Chapter Four: Despise Debt................55

Chapter Five: Demand Honest Money.........61

Chapter Six: Desire Peace with All
Nations..................................83

Chapter Seven: Disciple Others in
Liberty..................................97

The Unanimous Declaration
of the Thirteen United States of
America.................................109

The Constitution of the United States....117

The Bill of Rights.......................137

Bibliography.............................140

Endnotes.................................141

Introduction:

Christians at a Crossroads

Christian: A real disciple of Christ; one who believes in the truth of the Christian religion, and studies to follow the example, and obey the precepts, of Christ.

Patriot: A person who loves his country, and zealously supports and defends it and its interests.

-Webster's American Dictionary, 1828

"Liberty must at all hazards be supported. We have a right to it, derived from our Maker. But if we had not, our fathers have earned and bought it for us, at the expense of their ease, their estates, their pleasure, and their blood."

-John Adams

A Man at a Crossroads

I didn't care about politics.

Fourteen years ago, I was as an apathetic young Christian. I never voted in a single election. I didn't know anything about the issues. I didn't know who the candidates were, or how they got on the ballot.

Seven years later, I made a slight shift from apathetic young Christian to ambivalent young Pastor. I had mixed feelings about Christians being politically active. I still didn't really care about politics, but as a taxpayer with a family, apathy seemed irresponsible. However, I didn't want my political opinions, or lack thereof, to alienate anyone from the message I was called to preach: the Gospel. I decided that, at a minimum, I needed to vote.

I made sure I took the "proper" Christian Conservative positions on a handful of issues. I showed up at the polls on Election Day, I voted Republican, and I never preached politics from the pulpit. That's why, seven years later, I am as surprised as anyone about where God has led me.

Today, I am an activist. I am passionate about the issues. I have worked on political campaigns. I hold a leadership role in several political organizations. I speak publicly on the topics of faith and politics, the Constitution, economics, and personal liberty.

My journey from apathy to activism started with a series of questions: What is the Biblical balance between political activity and my Christian faith? Does the Bible command total submission to civil authorities? What do I

2

do when my conscience conflicts with the law? How can I know God's will for my life on the issue of politics?

Have you asked those questions too? As I searched the scriptures, I began to discover the answers, and they were very different from what I expected to find. I found answers that weren't being preached from the pulpits of American churches. Answers that changed my understanding of what it means to be a disciple of Jesus Christ.

That's why I wrote this book.

I was at a crossroads. I saw the corruption in our political system. I saw the lack of integrity in our leadership. I saw the betrayal of the American people by those they had trusted to protect them. As a citizen, I cared about my country, but as a Christian I knew it wasn't truly my home.

As Christians we live in a temporal world, but strive to be eternally minded. We try to strike a balance between being citizens of the United States, a nation that will one day pass away, and citizens of the Kingdom of God. We recognize that politics is not the solution to the sin problem of man, and it's not the vehicle through which Christ will restore His kingdom.

Still, our daily lives are governed by political power. It influences the condition of our neighborhoods, our cities, our states, and our nation. It affects our finances, our safety, and our children's future. We are faced with a choice: Do we have a responsibility to actively participate in the political process, or should we abstain?

DISCIPLE OF LIBERTY: SEVEN PRIORITIES OF A CHRISTIAN PATRIOT

We are not the first generation to find ourselves at this point of decision. Our nation's struggle for freedom began with a generation of people who were also faced with a choice.

Colonists at a Crossroads

In 1765, The Stamp Act was a tax imposed by British Parliament on the U.S. colonies. It required that most printed materials in the colonies carry a tax stamp. This was a revenue generating scheme that was meant to pay for British soldiers who remained in North America following the Seven Years War.

The British citizens weren't too keen on having standing armies on British soil, nor was Britain ready to continue paying the soldiers' salaries while they were stationed abroad. So, to avoid bringing fifteen hundred soldiers back to Britain unemployed, it was better to leave them across the pond to keep an eye on those pesky colonists. Since the colonists were the direct beneficiaries of the soldiers' presence, as they were a source of protection, it was only natural to charge the colonists for the soldiers' services. At least, that was the King's line of thinking.

King George used Writs of Assistance to enforce the Stamp Act. The Writs of Assistance were essentially transferable search warrants with no expiration date. They allowed British troops entry into private homes to make sure the colonists were complying with the Stamp Act. These violations of personal privacy turned many of the colonists against the British government. The Stamp Act is credited with bringing together numerous

4

underground patriot groups who opposed the growing tyranny of the Crown.

Before the Stamp Act, underground patriot groups such as the Sons of Liberty were peppered throughout the colonies but weren't coordinated in their efforts. As these groups began to work together toward repealing the Stamp Act, they set the stage for the next landmark in the American Revolution: The Boston Tea Party.

The Boston Tea Party was not all about tea. Though the Tea Act of 1773 served as the catalyst for the infamous act of rebellion, it actually reduced the price of tea for the colonists. Before the Tea Act, Great Britain had a monopoly on the tea going to the colonies. The Tea Act allowed the Dutch East India Company to export tea directly to the colonies, at a lower cost. However, there was still a three pence duty which was going straight to Great Britain, tacked on to the price of every pound of tea. That tax was the King's "cut," which was unacceptable to the colonists.

The colonists responded with an ultimatum. They gave the merchant's ships twenty-one days to leave port with their cargo and high tail it back across the Atlantic. Three of those ships, which had three hundred and forty-two chests of tea on board, refused to leave Boston Harbor.

The colonists were at a crossroads. It was time to put up or shut up. In front of seven thousand patriots gathered at the Old South Meeting House, Samuel Adams issued a rousing call to action. Adams said, "This meeting can do nothing further to save the country!" On that cue roughly one hundred colonists, disguised as Mohawk Indians,

5

boarded those ships in the Boston Harbor and tossed ninety-thousand pounds of tea into the water.

The Boston Tea Party wasn't an overnight rebellion. It was a green shoot sprouting from the seeds of liberty planted almost a decade before; seeds that started to take root with the Stamp Act of 1765. It wasn't really about the Tea Act. It wasn't even about the three pence levy on tea. Tea wasn't what drove a handful of rebels to dump three hundred and forty-two chests into the Boston Harbor and ultimately ignite the American Revolution. The Tea Party was simply the tipping point. It was the response to two key concerns in the hearts and minds of the colonists.

The first was Parliament's growing intrusion into the lives of the people.

The second was taxation without representation.

America at a Crossroads

I believe America has reached a second tipping point. Americans are angry. Americans are frustrated. They see the destruction of this country happening before their eyes, with breathtaking speed, and feel like there is nothing they can do to stop it. The deck seems to be stacked against the citizens, in favor of the politically connected. Career politicians do the bidding of special interests and fail to respond to the wishes of the constituents they were elected to represent.

When it comes time to cast our vote at the ballot box, our choices are nearly indistinguishable. In a nation of over three hundred million citizens, are these really the best candidates we can produce?

Tweedle-Dee or Tweedle-Dum.

Coke or Pepsi.

In the end, we somehow end up with more of the same rather than the "real change" promised by both sides of the aisle. Political insiders dominate Washington, and it's almost impossible for average Americans to run for office. Concerned citizens, who stand up and decide to make a difference, can't spare the time, or raise the necessary capital, to compete with the "chosen ones" who have political party backing. Even if we did have real choices for change, Congressional districts are rigged to ensure that the incumbents of Party X get into power, and stay there.

Here's the bad news: Those factors are what drive some Americans to just give up. Why try when it won't make a difference? One-third of all registered voters didn't even participate in the 2008 Presidential Election, and that's with a record turnout[1]. Our nation, which was supposed to be "of the People, for the People, and by the People," is unrecognizable when compared to the vision of our founders.

There's also good news: These factors are driving other Americans to take action, many for the first time in their lives. That's what brought us to our tipping point.

Instead of a tea tax, the healthcare issue has been the major catalyst for this new wave of activism. The debate over national healthcare reform has motivated a huge number of people to finally get involved, because now it's getting very personal.

Guess what? It's not really all about healthcare, any more than it was about tea two hundred and thirty-seven years ago. Healthcare is almost an afterthought when you listen to protestors speak their minds. Instead, they are talking about the Constitution, excessive taxes, personal liberty, and big government. It's the same two issues that the Boston Tea Party was really all about.

First, the federal government's growing intrusion into the lives of the people.

Second, taxation without representation.

The federal government's unconstitutional meddling in our lives has led many Americans to start asking questions. Just how far will we let the government reach? That is the question at the heart of the State Sovereignty movement, the Tea Party rallies, and the vocal opposition by average people to nearly every piece of legislation currently being proposed by Washington. Like the original Tea Party Patriots in 1773, average Americans are rising up to say, "No More!"

"Taxed Enough Already" is our "Taxation Without Representation." When hundreds to one were against TARP, sixty-seven percent were opposed to the GM takeover[2], and only thirty-seven percent supported the stimulus package[3], we are being taxed without our representation. In every case where the federal government is taking the hard earned dollars of American citizens and spending them on programs we do not support, it is taxation without representation. Whether it

8

is the latest bank bailout or "Cash For Clunkers," each of these measures is, in one way or another, a new tax on the American worker.

We have "representatives" but they do not truly represent us. The three thousand miles that separates some constituents from their member of Congress in Washington isn't much different from the three thousand miles that separated the colonists from their rulers in Britain. As citizens, we have lost our voice in Washington, and we know it.

Christians at a Crossroads

What about you? Have you called your Congressman, sent him e-mails and letters, and been ignored? Have you attended protests and rallies only to feel like the more noise you make, the less it seems to matter? Have the "seeds of liberty" begun to take root in your heart and mind?

You are not alone. Tens of thousands of people like you across the country, followers of Jesus Christ, are feeling compelled to get involved. They can't remain silent any more, and meetings can do nothing more to save our country. They're just not enough.

So where does that leave us? Christians in the midst of political unrest and turmoil. What is the proper response for a follower of Jesus Christ?

Within the church, there is vast disagreement over just how involved Christians should be in the political realm, and what the proper positions are on a number of issues. Some Christians are championing healthcare reform and social justice. They're advocating bigger government solutions to address the problems we face as a nation. Other Christians are championing personal responsibility and free-markets. They're advocating smaller government as the solution.

This idealogical rift is often accompanied by impassioned disagreement between brothers and sisters in Christ. Is it any wonder that so many Christians choose to stay uninvolved, and think it's best to remain silent?

Apathy, Ambivalence & Activism

Most Christians fall into three basic categories of involvement along the political spectrum: Apathy, Ambivalence, or Activism.

Apathy in politics is defined as inaction. Someone who is indifferent doesn't vote, sign petitions, put up yard signs, watch debates, or keep up with political news. People aren't always apathetic because they don't care. Sometimes they're apathetic because they feel like they can't make a difference.

To one degree or another, everyone is politically active. In politics, even the choice to do nothing has consequences. If you refuse to vote, refuse to sign a petition, or refuse to pay attention, it's political inaction that shifts a greater amount of power into the hands of a smaller number of people. People who choose to get involved.

Ambivalence is where most Christians fall when it comes to politics. Ambivalence is defined as having conflicting feelings about political action and politics as a whole. When it comes to voting, most Christians refuse to be apathetic because, frankly, it's politically incorrect not to vote. Wouldn't it be a bad testimony to our friends and neighbors if we simply abstained from voting all together? Even though it can be a hassle, and it's almost impossible to be informed on all the issues and candidates, it doesn't sit well with our conscience to stay home on Election Day. Many of us feel that voting is our reasonable service when it comes to political participation.

We cast our ballot without really knowing what, or who, we are voting for. When in doubt, we vote along party lines or according to our principles the best that we can. When it comes to politicians, we have to vote for someone. So we compromise, choosing the lesser of two evils. We "hold our noses" and pull the lever.

Getting involved in the primary process, on central committees, or any other level of activity outside of Election Day is simply out of the question. We've got too many commitments already, and when it comes to dividing our time between family, church, work and politics, politics loses every time.

Activism is another end of the spectrum. It's defined as going above and beyond our reasonable service of showing up at our assigned polling location every two or four years. Whether we are single issue activists, involved passionately in things we feel strongly about, or we feel called to run for office, activists are involved in doing something more than just the minimum.

As an activist, your yard may be full of political signs, your car covered in bumper stickers, and your radio constantly tuned to that all-talk station your teenager can't stand. Maybe you aren't a political "street evangelist," but have instead chosen "lifestyle evangelism," where you witness to family and friends through e-mail forwards or book recommendations.

Whether you are politically apathetic, politically active, or somewhere in the middle, it's your choice. No matter which category you're currently in, it's your liberty as a Christian and as an American. Jesus gives us no specific chapter and verse regarding the conduct and duty of a twenty-first century citizen living in a Constitutional Republic. You have the right to refuse to vote, stay uninformed, and abstain from politics all together. You have the right to cast your vote every four years, and leave it at that.

However, as the Apostle Paul observes, "All things are lawful, but not all things are profitable. All things are lawful, but not all things edify." In the area of politics, as with anything in the category of Christian liberty, we must determine which is the best choice. Which choice should we make for ourselves, for our family, for our nation, and for the sake of the Gospel?

What is God really calling us to do? To stand on the sidelines in apathy, and leave the future direction of this nation completely in the hands of the world? To straddle the fence of ambivalence, with just one foot gingerly placed in the political realm? Or, does God desire His

12

people to play a visible, active, and critical role at such a time as this? Those are the questions I hope to answer in this book.

Are you at a crossroads between apathy and activism? Then you're ready to discover the seven priorities of a Christian Patriot.

Chapter One:

Define the Limits of Authority

"The powers delegated by the proposed Constitution to the federal government are few and defined. Those which are to remain in the State governments are numerous and indefinite."

-James Madison

"The Constitution is not an instrument for the government to restrain the people, it is an instrument for the people to restrain the government-lest it come to dominate our lives and interests."

-Patrick Henry

Is Government Authority Unlimited?

Here's the thing about authority. There is only one entity in the universe whose authority is unlimited, and it's God. All others who have authority are bound by limits. Consider for a moment that even Satan, arguably the second most powerful being in the universe, only had limited authority to meddle with Job's life. Authority must have boundaries to maintain a free society. There is a word used to describe when people have unlimited authority:

It is *tyranny*.

Human authority, even when ordained by God, always has limits. A father has limits to his authority in disciplining his children. Though a parent may choose to use the "rod of correction" for a spanking, it's not a license for physical abuse. A police officer has limits to his authority regarding a suspect. During a traffic stop, there are procedures that must be followed. It would be an abuse of power to shoot first, and ask questions later. Our society functions best when the boundaries of authority are defined and obeyed. To identify when government has overstepped its boundaries, we must first define the limits of authority.

Is Christian Submission Unconditional?

The New Testament addresses the conduct of a Christian in relationship to government in Romans 13:1-7:

"Let every soul be subject unto the higher powers. For there is no power but of God: the powers that be are ordained of God. Whosoever therefore resisteth the power, resisteth the ordinance of God: and they that resist shall receive to themselves damnation...Wherefore ye must needs be subject, not only for wrath, but also for conscience sake."

You might be thinking, "Case closed. It's right there in Romans 13. The Bible teaches complete submission to authority. God, in His sovereignty, raises up rulers, both good and bad over nations. It isn't biblical for Christians to question the government, to criticize the President, or refuse to obey the law." Not only have I heard this objection frequently, but as a Pastor, I used to teach it. It's a common response to the suggestion that, as Thomas Jefferson memorably stated: "Resistance to tyrants is obedience to God!"

The Example of the Saints

The Bible does not teach complete, unconditional obedience to civil authority. History is full of examples where God's people were compelled to rebel. Both the Old and New Testament contain examples of God's people refusing to submit to authority, yet remaining righteous before God.

Were the Hebrew midwives in submission to authority when they disobeyed the King of Egypt, and refused to kill newborn males? (Exodus 1)

Was Rahab in submission to authority when she lied to the King of Jericho, and hid the Israeli spies? (Joshua 2)

Was David in submission to authority when he refused to surrender to Saul? (1 Samuel 23)

Was Elijah in submission to authority when he openly challenged Ahab and Jezebel? (1 Kings 21)

Were Shadrach, Meshach and Abednego in submission to authority when they refused to bow to the image of gold? (Daniel 3)

Was Daniel in submission to authority when he disobeyed the king's law forbidding prayer? (Daniel 6)

Was John the Baptist in submission to authority when he publicly scolded King Herod for his infidelity? (Matthew 14)

Were the Apostles in submission to authority when they refused to stop preaching on the streets of Jerusalem? (Acts 4)

Nearly every apostle of Jesus Christ was killed by the authorities whom they opposed. Christians throughout history have been imprisoned, tortured, and murdered by civil governments for refusing to submit to their laws.

Were these Christians in violation of God's principle of submission to authority? The scriptures commend these saints as examples of faith in action. They obeyed conscience rather than man, often with severe consequences. Clearly, resistance to civil laws is acceptable to God in some circumstances.

The Example of the Founders

For over a hundred years after the founding of this nation, the United States served as a beacon of liberty and an example of Christian principles in action. The foundation of our legal system is rooted firmly in Biblical principles of justice, equality, and human rights. America has been blessed in every way by God, and for decades served as a launching pad for world missions. Yet, this nation was conceived in an act of rebellion against a governing authority. Was the American Revolution an act of rebellion toward God?

If the American Revolution began as a bold rejection of God's Word, why did He give victory to the outnumbered and outgunned colonists against the British military? Why did God continue to bless this nation, and use this nation, to carry out His eternal purposes of worldwide evangelism? In other words, can a bad tree produce good fruits? Did God approve of the founding generation's rejection of British authority, or did He see it as a sin?

Whatever God's opinion was of the American Revolution, He ultimately granted victory to the colonists and established America as a free nation. The U.S. Constitution declares, and most people would agree, that our freedom is a national blessing to be preserved. That freedom wasn't established for our enjoyment alone, but also for our posterity. As the stewards of that blessing, don't we have a responsibility to "pay it forward?" If we don't preserve the blessing of liberty for our children, then we are handing them the curse of tyranny.

Rebellion was the Last Resort

Our founders didn't just pick up guns and start a war with Great Britain. They didn't even want a war in the first place. In 1776, the colonists were still British subjects, and King George the Third was still in authority. After years of abusive policies, like the Stamp Act and the Writs of Assistance, the thirteen colonies were ready to end their relationship with Great Britain. In the summer of 1776, fifty-six men representing the thirteen colonies, signed their names to the bottom of the most famous "Dear John" letter in the history of the world. This breakup letter is called the Declaration of Independence.

The Declaration was an attempt to bring a peaceful end to an abusive relationship. It begins with the following statement: "When in the Course of human events it becomes necessary for one people to dissolve the political bands which have connected them with another and to assume among the powers of the earth, the separate and equal station to which the Laws of Nature and of Nature's God entitle them, a decent respect to the opinions of mankind requires that they should declare the causes which impel them to the separation."

In other words, "Great Britain, things just aren't working out. It's not us, it's you, and it's time we started dating another form of government." The colonists weren't rebelling for sake of rebellion. They had a long list of complaints. These weren't your usual relationship struggles, like leaving the toilet seat up, or hogging the remote control. The colonists believed that their natural, God-given rights were being violated by the very government that was established to protect them.

20

The Declaration continues: "We hold these truths to be self-evident, that all men are created equal, that they are endowed by their Creator with certain unalienable Rights, that among these are Life, Liberty and the pursuit of Happiness. That to secure these rights, Governments are instituted among Men, deriving their just powers from the consent of the governed."

Our founders weren't just an ungrateful bunch of colonists seeking emancipation from the mother country. Their grievances addressed severe violations of the cosmic code of conduct, established by the one true Creator God of the universe. God, not government, created men equal, and endowed them with the right to life, liberty, and the pursuit of happiness.

This God-given right to pursue happiness wasn't understood to be a hedonistic license for a man to do what's right in his own eyes, at the expense of society at large. Our founders believed that to obtain individual and national happiness, it was necessary to demonstrate individual and national virtue. The pursuit of happiness may be best understood as the individual right for people to do whatever is necessary to better their life on Earth, so long as they don't trespass on anyone else's rights in the process.

The signers of the Declaration also believed that in the hierarchy of relationships, God holds the highest station of authority. After that, the individual. Finally, government, which is established to protect man's God-given rights. Government gets its power from the consent of the people.

These ideas were not new. Not only are they self-evident truths etched upon the souls of men, but they were also foundational ideas of British governance, dating all the way back to the Magna Carta of 1215, the Petition of Rights of 1628, and the English Bill of Rights of 1689. The Declaration of Independence was simply the latest contribution to a collection of documents which have articulated the philosophy of natural rights throughout western history.

Ultimately, the colonists were only insisting that they be allowed to have the same rights as every other British citizen. The Declaration goes on to list the "Twenty-Seven Dimensions of Incompatibility" which itemized their reasons for seeking separation. Some of the highlights were burdensome taxes, rigged trials, trumped up charges, destruction of property, threats of violence, and standing armies. It was a train of abuses and usurpations that had gone on for far too long.

The colonists reminded the King that this was not the first time that they had made their grievances known: "In every stage of these Oppressions We have Petitioned for Redress in the most humble terms: Our repeated Petitions have been answered only by repeated injury." Rebellion was not their preferred method of conflict resolution. Numerous appeals had been made. These petitions hadn't just been ignored, they were answered with an increasing level of tyranny. The King had ceased to act as the protector of their natural rights, and had ceased to rule for the good of the people.

The founders concluded, "A Prince, whose character is thus marked by every act which may define a Tyrant, is unfit to be the ruler of a free people." It was time for the colonists to exercise their right and duty to "throw off such Government, and to provide new Guards for their future security."

The Responsibility of a Ruler

The Bible isn't limited to giving instruction to citizens regarding obedience to their God-given authorities. It also has something to say about the character of rulers, and the legitimate function of a God-ordained government. Romans 13 provides a code of conduct that those in positions of authority are expected to obey:

> "For rulers are not a terror to good works, but to the evil. Wilt thou then not be afraid of the power? do that which is good, and thou shalt have praise of the same: For he is the minister of God to thee for good. But if thou do that which is evil, be afraid; for he beareth not the sword in vain: for he is the minister of God, a revenger to execute wrath upon him that doeth evil."

This passage identifies the kind of ruler who is a minister of God. It's a ruler who gives praise to the good, and executes wrath on the evil.

What about a ruler who, instead of executing wrath upon the evil, showers tyranny upon the good? What can be said of a ruler when, instead of being a terror to evil works, he becomes the enemy of good works? Is that ruler still the minister of God?

Even 1 Peter 2:13-14, which teaches submission to every ordinance, to governors, and to kings, is balanced with the idea that these human authorities have a responsibility to rule righteously. "Submit yourselves to every ordinance of man for the Lord's sake: whether it be to the king, as supreme; Or unto governors, as unto them that are sent by him for the punishment of evildoers, and for the praise of them that do well."

The majority of the text of the Declaration of Independence is filled with specific examples of the King's failure to govern righteously as the protector of the people's rights. Our founders were compelled by conscience to rebel.

Our Governing Authority

Here, in twenty-first century America, we are hundreds of years removed from King George the Third. Whatever authority he once held over this country is gone. In a Constitutional Republic, what is the "higher power" to which every soul is commanded to be in subjection? Is it the President, Congress, or the Supreme Court?

While these public servants and institutions certainly have authority under the law, and they "beareth not the sword in vain," they are not the law itself. In our Constitutional Republic, there is an authority higher than those who hold office. Our elected representatives swear an oath to that higher authority. It's an oath to uphold and defend that authority from enemies foreign and domestic.

24

The higher authority is the U.S. Constitution. The Constitution is the supreme law of the land. 1 Peter 2:13 teaches submission to every ordinance of man, and the Constitution is the place to start. It is the ultimate "ordinance of man." It's the foundation of every legitimate law in this country.

It's no mistake that the United States does not have a king. Even the President is just an employee of the people. The Constitutional separation of powers was specifically established to prevent the Executive Branch from exercising the role of a monarch. The founders of this nation did everything in their power to make it clear that the United States would have no king. They specifically sought to turn history upside-down when they designed a system where the government works for the people, and not the other way around. Our elected representatives may act as though they are royalty, but nothing could be further from the truth.

To really put this into context, imagine you are a business owner. You have a number of employees, and a manager who run things in your absence. No matter how many hours that manager works, and no matter how much authority you give him to administrate the business, he is not the owner. The manager only has as much authority as you give him. He still has to answer to you. He still has to obey you. He still depends on you for a paycheck.

If that manager engages in activities that damage the reputation of your business, or embezzles your money, or tries to usurp your authority, you have the right to fire him. If the damage he's done turns out to be irreparable, it's your right to fire everyone, shut down the whole

25

business, and start a new one. You are responsible to clean up the mess.

Likewise, the Constitution is the contract between the owners of this nation, the people, and the hired managers, our elected officials. The Constitution is the employee handbook. Any deviation our employees make from the specific, delegated duties described in that handbook is grounds for termination.

As Congress is the branch of government that is closest to the people, it was vested with the most power of all three branches. Even so, the Constitution delegates only a very limited and defined set of powers to Congress. The powers delegated to Congress are in Article I, Section 8. The Executive Branch has fewer enumerated powers, found in Article II, Section 2. The Judicial Branch has the fewest enumerated powers, found in Article I, Section 3, and Article III, Section 2.

The founders were so careful to make sure that there would be no future misunderstanding about the limited scope of power granted to the federal government, the Ninth Amendment was added which states: "The enumeration in the Constitution, of certain rights, shall not be construed to deny or disparage others retained by the people." In other words, when it comes to the people's rights, the Constitution isn't all inclusive: the framers didn't list every human right that the people possessed.

The Tenth Amendment was also added, which states: "The powers not delegated to the United States by the Constitution, nor prohibited by it to the States, are reserved to the States respectively, or to the people." In other words, when it comes to the federal government, the Constitution is exclusive: if the framers didn't specifically grant a power to the federal government in the text of the document, then the government doesn't have that power.

It's true that throughout history, God has established different forms of government in different nations at different times. He has raised nations up, and brought nations down. He has used tyrants from other nations to come in and overthrow the rulers of free people. So far, that has not happened here. As Christians in America, we are not called to answer for the conduct of citizens under another form of government, in another nation, at a different time in history. We are called to give an account for our conduct, in this nation, under this government, at this time in history.

In the United States, our form of government is a Constitutional Republic. Though some of our elected officials have undermined it, ignored it, and trampled it beneath their feet, the Constitution has not been abolished or legally overturned. It isn't even within the scope of Congress' authority to overturn the Constitution. Only the people have the right to do that.

The Declaration of Independence says that whenever any form of government becomes destructive to the unalienable rights of man, "it is the Right of the People to alter or abolish it, and to institute a new Government, laying its foundation on such principles and organizing its powers in such form, as to them shall seem most likely to effect their Safety and Happiness." Until that day arrives, our consent is what forms the foundation of legitimate government authority.

The Constitution is the God-ordained higher authority to which our elected officials must submit. Their responsibility is to protect it, defend it, and see to it that our liberties are secure. Our responsibility is to hold them accountable.

Chapter Two:

Demand Fidelity to the Constitution

"In questions of power then, let no more be heard of confidence in man but bind him down from mischief by the chains of the Constitution."

-Thomas Jefferson

"Extremism in the defense of liberty is no vice. Moderation in the pursuit of justice is no virtue."

-Barry Goldwater

Constitutional Consistency

Is it really such a radical idea to demand Constitutional consistency from every elected official, regardless of political party? To put it in a different context, does your spouse prefer that you are completely faithful, or mostly faithful? The Constitution is a contract between the government and the people. Only complete faithfulness is acceptable. The limits established in the Constitution are what protect us from the natural propensity for government to increase its power at our expense.

The boundaries in the Constitution provide for our security against the threat of politicians who might undermine our liberty through unconstitutional legislation. Overgrown and unconstitutional government comes at us from both sides of the political aisle. As George Washington observed, "However [political parties] may now and then answer popular ends, they are likely in the course of time and things, to become potent engines, by which cunning, ambitious, and unprincipled men will be enabled to subvert the power of the people and to usurp for themselves the reins of government, destroying afterwards the very engines which have lifted them to unjust dominion." Eventually, political parties and politicians forget to whom they really answer.

The problem with power is that is attracts exactly the kind of people who are likely to abuse it. Rhetoric aside, Republicans are just as guilty as Democrats when it comes to subverting the power of the people. John Adams said, "There is danger from all men. The only maxim of a free government ought to be to trust no man living with power to endanger the public liberty."

30

The Constitution was designed to be a well-forged set of chains, but not for the people. The Constitution does not steal away our freedoms. It binds the hands of the federal government to keep them out of mischief. The enumerated powers of the U.S. Constitution, along with the Bill of Rights, is how the founders tried to politician-proof our Republic.

Despite their attempt to be specific about the boundaries of government, somehow it wasn't enough. Did they underestimate the ambition of unprincipled men? No matter how cunning, ambitious, or unprincipled our elected officials may be, they have no excuse for overstepping their Constitutional bounds. Being faithful to the Constitution is the highest priority.

The Oath of Office for the President of the United States is specified in Article II, Section 1 of the Constitution: "I do solemnly swear (or affirm) that I will faithfully execute the Office of President of the United States, and will to the best of my Ability, preserve, protect and defend the Constitution of the United States." The Oath of Office for members of Congress is slightly different, but similar in principle: "I do solemnly swear (or affirm) that I will support and defend the Constitution of the United States against all enemies, foreign and domestic; that I will bear true faith and allegiance to the same; that I take this obligation freely, without any mental reservation or purpose of evasion; and that I will well and faithfully discharge the duties of the office on which I am about to enter. So help me God." This oath is also taken by the Vice President, members of the Cabinet, and all other civil and military officers and federal employees.

Romans 13 Revisited

Members of Congress do not swear loyalty to the President. The President does not swear allegiance to the Supreme Court. The sole duty of our elected officials is to protect, preserve and defend the Constitution against all enemies, foreign and domestic. So, if we really want to understand how Romans 13 applies in the United States today, we cannot ignore the weight of responsibility this Oath of Office carries for those who take it.

Pastor Chuck Baldwin offers the following rendering:

> "Let every soul be subject unto the [U.S. Constitution.] For there is no [Constitution] but of God: the [Constitution] that be [is] ordained of God. Whosoever therefore resisteth the [Constitution], resisteth the ordinance of God: and they that resist shall receive to themselves damnation. For [the Constitution is] not a terror to good works, but to the evil. Wilt thou then not be afraid of the [Constitution]? do that which is good, and thou shalt have praise of the same: For [the Constitution] is the minister of God to thee for good. But if thou do that which is evil, be afraid; for [the Constitution] beareth not the sword in vain: for [the Constitution] is the minister of God, a revenger to execute wrath upon him that doeth evil. Wherefore ye must needs be subject, not only for wrath, but also for conscience sake."

In this light, Romans 13 stands as a warning to those who seek the office of public service, and swear an oath before God and men to faithfully carry it out. Those who vow to uphold and defend the Constitution of the United States, only to break that vow to appease special interests, line their pockets, or guarantee themselves a victory in a future election, should beware. God says, "You will receive damnation."

In our Constitutional Republic, the warning of Romans 13 has incredible ramifications for our elected officials. They are called to obedience. They have a responsibility to administrate in a just and virtuous manner, as the ministers of God, not the ministers of unrighteousness. They are required to protect those who seek to do good, and to punish those who do evil. When those ministers cease to be righteous, and use their power on those they have been entrusted to serve, they cease to be the ministers of God. They become the enemies to the Constitution, obstacles to freedom, and tyrants to a nation. There is a word used to describe when our government managers violate their contract with the people:

It is *treason*.[4]

Our founders recognized that the enemies of liberty would often be the very individuals that were elected to protect it. They recognized that government itself posed the greatest threat to our freedom, and that the citizens must always be vigilant. That's why Jefferson reminds us, "Every government degenerates when trusted to the rulers of the people alone. The people themselves, therefore, are its only safe depositories." How can we expect our representatives to take the Constitution seriously, if we remain silent in the face of abuse? What good is a Constitution without accountability?

Conservative Inconsistencies

It's amazing how many conservatives, currently voicing their disapproval of President Obama's policies, remained silent as George W. Bush committed a long train of abuses against the Constitution. Whether they allowed this because Bush was "one of them," a professing Christian and Republican, or simply out of fear and the need for security in the wake of September 11th, conservatives in America surrendered many precious liberties for a little temporary safety.

Under the Bush administration, America got The Patriot Act, a bill that was posted on the intranet of the House of Representatives just fifteen minutes before it was voted on. This was a bill that not a single House member had read in its entirety before being passed by an overwhelming majority. It's a bill that violates at least two of the first ten amendments[5]. Where was the outcry from conservatives then?

America also got The John Warner Defense Authorization Act, which gives the President the power to declare a national emergency, and station troops anywhere in the United States to "restore public order." The far-reaching and vague language of this bill gives the Executive Branch power to declare martial law if there is a natural disaster, public health emergency, terrorist incident, or "other condition.[6]" Would this expansion of police-state power go unchallenged if proposed by Barack Obama today?

Many of the powers seized by the Bush administration have now been handed over to the Obama administration.

34

Freedoms we choose to surrender under one administration are seldom handed back to us by the next. These unconstitutional power-grabs should concern Republicans and Democrats alike. Democrats who are so eager to give the government full access to their medical records for the sake of healthcare reform, may not be so excited once a Republican gets into office.

Original Intent

When it comes to examining any issue, or proposed legislation, the primary criteria of consideration should be this: Is it Constitutional? You don't need to be a legal expert to determine if proposed legislation falls within the enumerated powers granted to the federal government in the Constitution. Consider Thomas Jefferson's opinion on the matter:

> "I consider the foundation of the Constitution as laid on this ground that 'all powers not delegated to the United States, by the Constitution, nor prohibited by it to the states, are reserved to the states or to the people.' To take a single step beyond the boundaries thus specially drawn around the powers of Congress, is to take possession of a boundless field of power, not longer susceptible of any definition."

Jefferson feared that even a small step beyond the enumerated powers in the U.S. Constitution would open up a Pandora's Box of potential abuses by the federal government. Once the federal government was allowed to expand the scope of its power beyond the very specific

DISCIPLE OF LIBERTY: SEVEN PRIORITIES OF A CHRISTIAN PATRIOT

boundaries described in the text of the Constitution, there would be little hope that the people could prevent federal intrusion into any area that it wished to intervene. History has proven that these fears were not misplaced.

Jefferson also recognized the importance of future generations understanding the context in which the Constitution was written and ratified. Even as early as 1819[7], there were those who wanted to argue for a "living" Constitution which could be reinterpreted and rewritten to suit the needs of those in power. Jefferson insisted that when it came to understanding the meaning of any portion of the Constitution, is was best to "carry ourselves back to the time when the Constitution was adopted, recollect the spirit manifested in the debates and instead of trying what meaning may be squeezed out of the text or invented against it, conform to the probable one in which it was passed."

He was not alone in this opinion. James Madison agreed, "I entirely concur in the propriety of resorting to the sense in which the Constitution was accepted and ratified by the nation. In that sense alone it is the legitimate Constitution. If that is not the guide in expounding it, there may be no security." A literal interpretation of the Constitution, consistent with intent of those who drafted it, is the only interpretation which guarantees the security of the people in this nation.

Today we are dealing with the realization of what Alexander Hamilton called the "implied powers" of the Constitution. Hamilton contended that the federal government could loosely interpret the Constitution when necessary, and exercise powers that were reasonably

36

suggested in the Constitution. His doctrine of implied powers gave birth to the idea of the so-called living Constitution, which has led to numerous expansions of federal power. Specifically, the General Welfare and the Commerce Clauses of the Constitution have been expanded beyond what the framers ever envisioned. This has been a Trojan Horse which has undermined states' rights and individual liberty ever since. Now, anything that can be remotely connected to the "general welfare" and "commerce" has become a target of federal regulation.

However, even Alexander Hamilton, a proponent of a strong, centralized government, acknowledged that there were Constitutional lines that should never be crossed. When they were crossed, it was up to the people to take corrective measures. He said, "If the federal government should overpass the just bounds of its authority and make a tyrannical use of its powers, the people, whose creature it is, must appeal to the standard they have formed, and take such measures to redress the injury done to the Constitution as the exigency may suggest and prudence justify."

In other words, the creation is not greater than the creator. The states gave birth to the federal government, not the other way around. The Constitution is clear that all powers not delegated to the federal government have been reserved to the states and the people. Yet, this principle has been completely reversed over the last one hundred and fifty years. The federal government now operates as if its powers are numerous and indefinite. The states are treated like the redheaded stepchildren.

Constitutional Flexibility

While the Constitution is certainly not a malleable lump of clay in the hands of politicians, it is also not written in stone. The founders understood that things can change, and that they might have missed something along the way. That's why they provided a process by which it can be legally amended. The basis of our political system is the right of the people to alter, or even abolish, the current form of government. As Washington observed in his farewell address, "The Constitution which at any time exists, 'till changed by an explicit and authentic act of the whole People, is sacredly obligatory upon all."

The Constitution, as it stands right now, is the Constitution to which our elected officials are bound. If it needs to be changed, it must be amended. It's an arduous process that cannot be rammed through at one o'clock in the morning, while the American people sleep. That's why some legislators don't like the amendment process very much. This was designed to be one of the protective characteristics of a Republic. Thomas Jefferson reminds us, "Although a republican government is slow to move, yet when once in motion, its momentum becomes irresistible." In most cases legislative gridlock is good. Dramatic changes to our Republic aren't supposed to be easy to accomplish.

Many politicians simply don't care whether proposed legislation meets the founders' strict criteria on Constitutionality. The proverbial camel's nose went under the tent flap long ago. We have been living under hundreds of unconstitutional laws for decades, and unconstitutional legislation is still frequently passed. We

38

aren't likely to roll back decades of bad legislation in one fail swoop anytime soon.

Our Responsibility

Even if our representatives don't care about their oath of office, a written Constitution gives us a standard by which we can hold our representatives accountable. It's up to us to use the Constitution as a bludgeon to beat back the encroachments of liberty and the overreach of federal power. It's up to us to enforce their contract with the American people. We must demand fidelity.

Why do we allow our elected officials to violate their oaths of office? We would never tolerate such behavior from our employees. Why do we remain silent when it's happening at the highest level of government? As Christians we are called to be the light of the world, exposing unrighteousness and darkness wherever it is found. Are the Oval Office and the Halls of Congress beyond the reach of the light of truth?

Our founders believed that government could only be trusted to preserve freedom and liberty under the watchful eye of "we the people." If our elected officials believe that they can break their contract with us, since we haven't forced them to answer to us, then we are partially to blame. We were the stewards of liberty, and we stopped paying attention.

That's not to say that our representatives aren't to blame for government gone wild. Tyranny is a byproduct of bipartisan schemes. Both parties have engaged in a long campaign to erode our Constitutional rights. Our representatives have strayed from the Constitutional principles they vowed to uphold. Principles they vowed to defend. Principles that must never be abandoned.

There is no excuse for Republicans or Democrats who have blatantly violated their oath to uphold and defend the Constitution. When politicians sacrifice sacred principles for political purposes, it is not only our right, it is our duty, to hold them accountable. It is up to us to reassert the principles of liberty that form the foundation and heritage of our freedom.

Our heritage of freedom and liberty declares that individuals have certain unalienable rights, and that these rights cannot be taken away. If we are going to hold our representatives accountable, then we must oppose laws which expand government beyond its Constitutional limits. We must oppose laws which restrict a law-abiding citizen's right to keep and bear arms. We must oppose laws which obstruct our right to free speech.

Our heritage of freedom and liberty declares that the checks and balances established by our Constitution are necessary to ensure that our government stays limited in scope. Therefore, we must oppose appointing judges who invent laws and dictate social policy. We must oppose lawmakers passing bills before they have even read them. We must oppose legislation that does not apply to certain elected officials.

Our heritage of freedom and liberty declares that the protection of private property and the preservation of free markets is essential to our prosperity and freedom. Therefore, we must oppose government ownership or

40

control over private businesses. We must oppose legislation that allows the confiscation of private property.

Our heritage of freedom and liberty declares that reckless government spending hurts our economy and condemns people to a form of oppression through inflation, debt, and higher taxes. Therefore, we must oppose the confiscation of our wealth through burdensome taxation. We must oppose the destruction of our savings through inflation. We must oppose deficit spending which saddles future generations with debts that can never be repaid. We must oppose the forced transfer of wealth from those who have earned it to those who have not.

These aren't just conservative principles. These are American principles, espoused by our founders. These are the principles that make up the fabric of our Constitutional Republic. Only by insisting that our leaders honor their oath to uphold and defend the Constitution can we ensure that America remains a land of freedom and opportunity, where ordinary people can do extraordinary things. A land where we have the freedom to make our own decisions, without government intrusion, on matters such as our religion, our health care, our property, and our children's education.

It's up to us, Christian Patriots, to lead the way by demanding accountability and fidelity to the Constitution. It is the "higher authority" that God has established as the law of the land. Only through demanding impartial, consistent, and unconditional fidelity to the Constitution can we ensure that our liberties, and the liberties of all people, are secure.

Chapter Three:

Defend Liberty for All People

"The God who gave us life gave us liberty at the same time; the hand of force may destroy, but cannot disjoin them."

-Thomas Jefferson

"Now the Lord is that Spirit: and where the Spirit of the Lord is, there is liberty."

-2 Corinthians 3:17

The Tree of Liberty

God is the Author of Liberty. The Bible is the story of how mankind traded a life of freedom and blessing for the curse and bondage of sin. It took place beneath a tree. It's also the story of how Jesus Christ embarked on a search and rescue mission to restore that freedom to mankind. He ransomed the souls of men taken captive by a tyrant. He restored the broken relationship between the Creator and His creation. That restoration took place upon a tree.

We are hard-wired with a desire to be free. That desire goes all the way back to the Garden of Eden. When Jesus came to Earth and proclaimed liberty to the captives, it wasn't a political campaign. He came to address a spiritual problem. All the freedom in the world means nothing if we come to the end of our life on this Earth spiritually dead, and condemned to an eternity separated from our Creator God. That's why Jesus was nailed to the cross, the true Tree of Liberty. He was buried and rose from the grave, fulfilling ancient prophecy, so that we could all be eternally free.

Canadian politician Thomas Reed said, "One of the greatest delusions in the world is the hope that the evils of the world are to be cured by legislation." If we want to cure the evils of the world, the Gospel offers a genuine hope that we will never find on an election ballot.

While politics is not the solution to man's sin problem, the death of Christ didn't erase the consequences of sin, or cure the depravity of lost men. Until Jesus returns, there will be wars, injustice, corruption, and death. As a

44

Christian Patriot, we should strive to have a balanced view of what can be accomplished through the political process, and what can only be accomplished through the blood of Christ.

God wants people to live in liberty. Consider that even on the issue of eternal salvation, God is not a cosmic arm-twister. He gives us the liberty to choose. Throughout the Bible when God's people were enslaved, He went to great lengths to set them free. Just ask Pharaoh.

It's also true that, throughout history, God has allowed conquering nations to bring His people under subjection. It's true that Christians across the globe have lived and died under harsh political regimes. God, in His sovereignty, and for His purposes, has allowed individuals and nations to live under tyranny. Not all of God's people have enjoyed the blessings of liberty.

However, we have been given the blessing of liberty. For over two hundred years, the United States has enjoyed the fruit of the Tree of Liberty planted by our founders. There is no evidence that our liberties are being taken away by the hand of God. Instead, the Tree of Liberty is under attack from a tyranny rising within our nation. Unrighteous men in powerful places have been hacking away at its branches while the American people have been fast asleep.

There was a physical elm tree in Boston that our founders called "the Liberty Tree." It was a rallying point for the colonists as their resistance to Britain began to grow. On August 14, 1765, the Sons of Liberty first gathered beneath this tree to protest the Stamp Act. They hung tax collectors in effigy from its branches. When they called a meeting, a yellow flag was flown from the Liberty Tree to signal the event. Eventually, the Sons of Liberty could be found scattered throughout every one of the colonies. They would identify a large tree, or erect a Liberty Pole, to be used as a meeting place. Those Liberty Trees were physical representations of the self-evident, unalienable, God-given rights of man that were being threatened by tyranny from abroad.

That's why the Liberty Tree was also the object of ridicule by British loyalists. At the Liberty Tree, British soldiers tarred and feathered colonists for opposing the Crown. In 1775, a group of loyalists cut down the Liberty Tree in Boston, and used it for firewood. This direct attack only further enraged the colonists. The image of the Liberty Tree was soon emblazoned upon the flags flown by the colonists to demonstrate their continued commitment to defend freedom. The Liberty Tree could not be hewn down or uprooted from their hearts and minds.

Preserving The Tree of Liberty

The colonists finally won their independence from Great Britain. Lives were lost and fortunes were spent, but when the American Revolution was over, our founders possessed freedom, one of the most valuable commodities on the face of the Earth. In a letter to James Monroe, James Madison wrote, "The eyes of the world being thus on our Country, it is put the more on its good behavior, and under the greater obligation also, to do justice to the Tree of Liberty by an exhibition of the fine fruits we gather from it." Our founders considered themselves stewards of that Tree, with a responsibility to ensure that every individual had equal access to its fruit: life, liberty, and the pursuit of happiness.

This was the beginning of the great American experiment in freedom called a Constitutional Republic. This experiment rested on the premise that governments are instituted among men for a specific purpose. According to Thomas Jefferson, "The care of human life and happiness, and not their destruction, is the first and only legitimate object of good government...The freedom and happiness of man...[are] the sole objects of all legitimate government."

John Adams agreed, "Government is instituted for the common good; for the protection, safety, prosperity, and happiness of the people; and not for profit, honor, or private interest of any one man, family, or class of men; therefore, the people alone have an incontestable, unalienable, and indefeasible right to institute government; and to reform, alter, or totally change the same, when their protection, safety, prosperity, and happiness require it."

Our founders handed us the stewardship of liberty, but liberty is truly the gift of God. Just as life is not ours to give up because it's source is beyond our humanity, our natural rights aren't ours to surrender through complacency or coercion. John Adams puts it this way: "If men through fear, fraud or mistake, should in terms renounce and give up any essential natural right, the eternal law of reason and the great end of society, would absolutely vacate such renunciation; the right to freedom being the gift of God Almighty, it is not in the power of

Man to alienate this gift, and voluntarily become a slave." Adams insisted, "Liberty must at all hazards be supported. We have a right to it, derived from our Maker. But if we had not, our fathers have earned and bought it for us, at the expense of their ease, their estates, their pleasure, and their blood."

The blessing of freedom is too valuable and rare to let the Tree of Liberty wither away. When Adams said that it must be supported "at all hazards," he meant no threat to liberty was too small to oppose, and no cost too great in opposing it. It's our duty to make sure that we can pass the baton to the next generation. It is our turn to lay our lives and fortunes on the line.

George Washington said, "The preservation of the sacred fire of liberty, and the destiny of the Republican model of government, are...finally staked, on the experiment entrusted to the hands of the American people." What would it say about us if we simply gave our freedom away? If through our apathy, we condemn our posterity to a life of heavy-handed tyranny, unconstitutional laws, burdensome taxes, and never-ending debt? It would be the height of selfishness to deny future generations the freedom and liberty that we have been blessed to enjoy.

The Enemies of the Tree of Liberty

Government itself can be the enemy of liberty when it strays beyond its Constitutional bounds. Thomas Jefferson lamented, "The natural progress of things is for liberty to yield and government to gain ground." The very institution which the founders established to be the

48

protector of liberty often poses the greatest threat to our freedom.

For decades, our federal government has worked in darkness, chipping away at our liberty while increasing its own power. James Madison warned, "There are more instances of the abridgment of the freedom of the people by the gradual and silent encroachment of those in power, than by sudden and violent usurpation."

This gradual process of subverting the Constitution is more dangerous than sudden usurpation because it goes unnoticed by the people much longer. Few conservatives complained while the Bush administration quietly seized many of our freedoms and expanded the deficit. Ironically, the Obama administration's swift restructuring of our Republic is fueling the opposition. It is obvious our liberties are being attacked.

Complacency is another enemy of liberty. Consider the words of American broadcast journalist Edward R. Murrow: "A nation of sheep will beget a government of wolves." We have allowed government to take our freedoms because for so long we just didn't care. Seduced by pleasure and entertainment, we convinced ourselves that politics and government would take care of themselves.

Thomas Paine reminds us, "Those who expect to reap the benefits of freedom must, like men, undergo the fatigue of supporting it." It's hard work being the watchdogs for our Republic. It takes time, energy, and resources to hold Congress accountable. With few exceptions, the mainstream media has done little to expose the real extent of government corruption, fraud, and waste. The burden falls upon us to take up the mantle that modern journalism has abandoned.

Fear is another enemy of liberty. 2 Timothy 1:7 reminds us that, "God hath not given us the spirit of fear; but of power, and of love, and of a sound mind." Fear and freedom cannot coexist. Most of us live in fear of everything from radical Muslims, to pot-smokers, to the ever present threat of a flu pandemic. The Republicans and Democrats use the politics of fear to scare us and divide us into warring factions and special interest groups. As a result, we ask government to legislate us to safety and protect us from everything we fear. We fear what our neighbor might do with too much freedom, more than we fear what our government might do with too much power.

Liberty for Our Enemies

If we want to remain free we have to resist the temptation to legislate liberties away from other citizens. We may fear them, or disagree with their choices, but as Thomas Paine reminds us, "He that would make his own liberty secure, must guard even his enemy from oppression; for if he violates this duty, he establishes a precedent that will reach to himself."

During World War I, President Wilson imprisoned up two thousand "anarchists" without trial, and without charges, for the remainder of the war. During World War II, over seventy-thousand American citizens were locked up by President Roosevelt, simply because they were Japanese[8]. American history is full of examples when, motivated by fear, citizens turned a blind eye to such abuses. Our

50

federal government clearly violated the Constitutional rights of these citizens who were declared "enemy combatants" or "threats" to the government.

The founders of this nation believed that the federal government was a greater threat to our freedom than any other threat at home or abroad. The Patriot Act is an unconstitutional law that gives federal agents the ability to write their own search warrants against anyone deemed an enemy combatant, sympathizer, or other term used to label those who dare to challenge the federal government. The Fourth Amendment was included in the Bill of Rights to protect us from this exact kind of activity. It was meant to guarantee that American citizens would have the Constitutional right to be left alone.

The vagueness of the language in legislation like the Patriot Act, coupled with the ever-changing definition of who constitutes an "enemy of the State," should make every American nervous. Many conservatives foolishly believe that these laws could never be used against them. They're just for the "bad guys." It only takes a few instances of "Christian" militia groups or radical Tea Party activists threatening violence before the Department of Homeland Security labels every one of us an "enemy combatant."

Rather than working to protect the liberties of others, out of fear we lobby government to make our personal preferences into law because certain activities offend us, or because we think it will make us safer. Instead of making us more secure, it does the opposite. Once we support taking freedoms away from someone, eventually someone else is going to come along and try to take away ours. It's just a matter of time before our behaviors are deemed offensive to someone, or we're labeled as dangerous. If the day comes when the Bible is outlawed, where public prayer is illegal, and where preaching on certain issues from the pulpit becomes a crime, it will only happen after we have participated in establishing the precedent for it.

Benjamin Franklin said, "They that can give up essential liberty to obtain a little temporary safety, deserve neither liberty nor safety." We live in a world of uncertainty and risk, where underwear bombers might board airplanes, and militia groups may plot a violent government takeover. What freedoms will we surrender to try to eliminate these fear-based possibilities? Are we willing to send our spouses and children through full body scanners, and allow federal agents to listen to our phone calls? Is the government's promise of safety worth giving up our defense against unlawful searches and seizures? Do we really want to head down that slippery slope where we allow our government to profile Americans based on age, race, ethnicity, or political beliefs?

Thomas Jefferson said, "I would rather be exposed to the inconveniences attending too much liberty than those attending too small a degree of it." Living in the kind of nation our founders envisioned comes with its share of inconveniences. It's been said that liberty may be a dangerous thing, but it is the safest thing we have. If you think liberty is inconvenient, wait until you try tyranny.

The enemies of liberty abound, but most aren't hiding in caves. Instead, our complacency, our fear, and even our own government, are greater threats to our freedom than anything else we face. We have to be vigilant in protecting the God-given rights of everyone, even people who may use that freedom in ways we don't condone. From the Methodist to the Atheist, from the Hispanic to the Arabic, we have to be diligent in defending the natural rights of every American. The only way to guarantee our own freedom is to ensure that the freedom of others is secure.

Chapter Four:

Despise Debt

"The rich rule over the poor, and the borrower is servant to the lender."

-Proverbs 22:7

"I place economy among the first and most important republican virtues, and public debt as the greatest of dangers to be feared."

-Thomas Jefferson

The Danger of Debt

Volumes have been written about the wisdom of avoiding debt when it comes to managing our personal affairs. While personal debt is not directly the focus of this chapter, the biblical principle of Proverbs 22:7 is true on a personal and national scale. Debt enslaves, and the solution to debt is simple: Don't spend money that you don't have.

Since average Americans live their lives buried up to their eyeballs in debt, many people are generally unconcerned that our federal government lives the same way. However, the consequences are incomparable. My personal debt rarely affects anyone other than my family and my creditors. Government debt is different because it has the power to enslave entire nations for generations to come. Thomas Jefferson observed, "The principle of spending money to be paid by posterity, under the name of funding, is but swindling futurity on a large scale." It is grand theft from our own grandchildren. We are currently stealing from them at an unprecedented rate.

In September 2009, the Obama administration projected a cumulative nine trillion dollar deficit between 2010 and 2019: a spending blitz that will push the national debt to over twenty-trillion dollars[9]. First of all, let's come to grips with the kind of numbers being discussed. Just one trillion dollars is a very large number. If it were possible to spend one million dollars a day from the birth of Jesus Christ to the present, you would only have spent about seven hundred and thirty-four billion dollars total. That's approximately the amount of money provided by

Congress to bail out Wall Street in a single bill, The Emergency Economic Stabilization Act of 2009.

This nine trillion dollar projection for the next ten years comes out to a staggering $2,465,753,424 per day for the next ten years. That's like charging two and one half billion dollars on our children's credit cards, every day, for the next 3,650 days.

News of this enormous deficit has Republicans up in arms, demonizing the Obama administration for reckless economic policies that are certain to destroy America. It is, without question, the most outrageous spending spree the federal government has ever embarked on in its two hundred and thirty-four years of existence. Barack Obama has secured his place as the biggest spender to ever occupy the Oval Office. George W. Bush will have to settle for second place[10].

Bush, Obama, and the Bailouts

For all their small government rhetoric, Republicans are almost as bad as Democrats when it comes to overspending and deficits. When Bush took office in 2001, the national debt ceiling was a mere six trillion dollars, which is less than half of what it is today[11]. By November 2004, the Bush administration had managed to escalate it to over eight trillion dollars, an increase of more than two trillion dollars in under four years. That's two and one half times the entire federal accumulated debt from 1776 to 1980[12]. In 2008, alone the national debt increased by a staggering one trillion dollars.

As outrageous as these numbers are, it doesn't even include the five trillion dollars in liabilities of Fannie Mae and Freddie Mac[13]. In the waning days of the Bush administration, these Government Sponsored Entities were taken into "conservatorship" through the Housing and Economic Recovery Act in July 2008, and the Federal Housing Finance Agency in September 2008. In other words, they were nationalized. Every dollar of exposure is a potential liability to the American taxpayer.

Conservatives who pine away for the more "frugal" years of prior Republican administrations may be surprised to find that, from 1980 to 1992, the national debt quadrupled from nine hundred and forty-billion to four trillion dollars[14].

When it comes to bailouts, the Obama administration is working hard not to be outdone by a Republican. Through February 2009, the U.S. government had already committed nearly ten trillion dollars to the bailouts, an amount that would have been sufficient to pay off more than ninety percent of the nation's mortgages. By March, the total estimate of government loans, spending, and guarantees was at thirteen trillion dollars, more money than the entire national debt[15]. In July 2009, Special Inspector General Neil Barofsky reported to Congress that the total potential cost of these bailouts exceeded twenty-three trillion dollars. That's more than the cost of the New Deal, World War II, and the moon landing combined[16].

If the borrower is servant to the lender, then our national debt has reached a point where it also poses a threat to our national sovereignty. In July 2009, China held eight hundred billion dollars worth of U.S. Treasuries[17]. The long term stability of our dollar now depends upon China's continued support of our government's spending habits. As Paul Craig Roberts, Assistant Secretary of the Treasury during the Reagan administration, observes, "A country whose financial affairs are in the hands of foreigners is not a superpower."

Render Unto Caesar?

No matter how hard we try, as individuals, to live a frugal lifestyle, we are forced to finance government waste. No matter how hard we try to eliminate personal debt, the federal government is driving us deeper into debt every day. Each citizen's share of the current national debt is forty-thousand dollars.

The problem isn't a shortage of taxes. Americans are taxed enough already. The average American currently works ninety-nine days out of every year just to pay their annual tax bill[18]. In 2009, the federal government collected just over two trillion dollars in revenue.

When Jesus says, "Render therefore unto Caesar the things which be Caesar's, and unto God the things which be God's" what exactly does that mean for us? Does Caesar have a rightful claim to thirty percent of our income? Does Caesar have the right to mortgage our future to the tune of forty-thousand dollars apiece? Can Caesar use that money in violation of the Constitution, to prop up failing businesses, and fund entitlement programs? At what point is Caesar laying claim to more than his "fair share?"

59

Remember, there is no Caesar in America. The power of the Republic was placed into the hands of the people. Our elected officials work for us. Yet, in our current recession, government jobs and salaries have increased, while real unemployment in the private sector exceeds ten percent. Big government acts like a parasite that siphons money from our pockets, making it harder for our families to make ends meet. We are forced to curb our lifestyles to fund Washington's excess.

Luke 16:11 says that the way we handle money is the true measure of responsibility. Our government's excessive spending and debt isn't congruent with the Christian values of stewardship and frugality. We have gotten so used to the idea that government is inefficient and wasteful, it's hardly more that a punchline in a Jay Leno monologue. It's no laughing matter when the Congress can't document where the stimulus money went. The joke is on us when the Federal Reserve won't reveal who was bailed out at the taxpayers' expense, at the height of the financial crisis[19].

We deserve answers.

If we want to fully understand the issue of government spending and debt, we must also examine our monetary system. The Federal Reserve has acted as an accomplice in all of this. So far they have escaped public scrutiny and blame, but the Federal Reserve stands at the center of every economic crisis in America for the last ninety-seven years. As Christian Patriots, we must not only make it a priority to despise government debt, but we must also make it a priority to demand honest money.

Chapter Five:

Demand Honest Money

"We are in danger of being overwhelmed with irredeemable paper, mere paper, representing not gold nor silver; no sir, representing nothing but broken promises, bad faith, bankrupt corporations, cheated creditors and a ruined people."

— Daniel Webster

"Divers weights are an abomination unto the LORD; and a false balance is not good."

-Proverbs 20:23

Understanding Money

Jesus frequently spoke about money. It's the subject of at least eleven out of thirty-nine parables. Our attitude concerning money, and our stewardship of money, has both temporal and eternal consequences. Money is so familiar to us, we hardly notice it. It represents half of every transaction in our economy. It's a fundamental component of American society. Some of us spend one-third of our waking lives working to earn it. Yet, most of us barely understand it.

John Adams stressed the importance of making sure American citizens were educated on the issue of money. In a letter to Thomas Jefferson, he wrote: "All the perplexities, confusions, and distress in America, arise, not from defects in their Constitution or Confederation, not from want of honor or virtue, so much as from downright ignorance of the nature of coin and credit, and circulation."

The Constitution is not perfect. It was crafted by flawed men. Washington D.C. will never be populated with angels. Politicians will always be susceptible to moral compromise and lapses of integrity. However, if we take Adams at his word, many of our nation's ills could be cured if we just understood the nature of money and banking. A basic understanding of sound money, and the nature of coin, credit, and circulation, is essential if we are to have honest government, and a free society.

Brief History of Money

Thousands of years ago money developed in the free-market as a way to facilitate exchange. Before the advent of money, two people had to have exactly each other wanted in order to complete a transaction. This is known as the double coincidence of wants. As economies became more complex through increased specialization in the division of labor, direct exchange became more difficult. Money was the solution. It allowed two people to engage in commerce with money as a substitutionary medium of exchange.

There is nothing magical about money. Money is simply the most marketable commodity in any society. Over time, gold and silver emerged as the preferred medium of exchange across cultures throughout the world. These precious metals were valuable for industry and jewelry. They possessed certain qualities that allowed them to be easily recognized, divided, and transported. In the contest of competing commodities, gold and silver won out as being best suited for money.

Money has always been subject to corruption. There have always been those who have sought to gain control of its production and circulation. Emperors and kings throughout history have found that taxation and borrowing were insufficient means of financing expansive empires. They often resorted to debasing the currency to expand the money supply and create personal slush funds. Coins were clipped or shaved to reduce their precious metal content. Base metals were sometimes added to dilute their purity, or paper money was issued and forced on the citizens by governmental decree.

Honest Money

The biblical warning against unjust weights and measures was a warning against tampering with the system of commerce and exchange. In ancient times, sellers in the marketplace used scales to verify the amount and weight of their goods. Unscrupulous sellers would tamper with the scales passing off a smaller amount for a larger, yet charging the same price.

Just weights and measures is the subject of Leviticus 19:35-36: "Ye shall do no unrighteousness in judgment, in meteyard, in weight, or in measure. Just balances, just weights, a just ephah, and a just hin, shall ye have: I am the LORD your God, which brought you out of the land of Egypt." Constitutional money adheres to this biblical precept. Nobody questions the fact that a pound should be sixteen ounces, and an ounce should be 28.35 grams. The dollar is also a unit of measure. When the Coinage Act of 1792 was passed, the definition of a dollar was 371.25 grains of pure silver. The true definition of a dollar cannot be changed any more than an inch can be shortened or a pound can be lightened. Nevertheless, the practical definition of a dollar has changed as currency debasement has depreciated its purchasing power.

With the appearance of paper money, inflation and currency debasement became much easier to achieve. Printing presses can produce currency much faster than gold mining and minting for a fraction of the cost. The framers of our Constitution were well acquainted with these schemes and did everything they could to ensure that the United States was founded on the principles of honest money.

64

Benjamin Franklin believed that the colonies would have borne a little tax on tea and other nuisances had they been allowed to operate an independent money system: "The refusal of King George III to allow the colonies to operate an honest money system, which freed the ordinary man from the clutches of the money manipulators, was probably the prime cause of the revolution."

George Washington recognized that the lure of easy money and credit would always be a temptation that could lead our nation astray from its founding principles. He warned that if "we should unfortunately stumble again on unfunded paper money or any similar species of fraud, we shall assuredly give a fatal stab to our national credit in its infancy. Paper money will invariably operate in the body of politics as spirit liquors on the human body. They prey on the vitals and ultimately destroy them. Paper money has had the effect in your state that it will ever have, to ruin commerce, oppress the honest, and open the door to every species of fraud and injustice."

Constitutional Money

Paper money has the destructive potential to ruin commerce, oppress the honest, and open the door to fraud and injustice. The founders were so certain of this that they placed specific language in the Constitution to prevent a reckless monetary policy from endangering the future of the nation.

Article I, Section 8 of the U.S. Constitution enumerates the powers of Congress when it comes to money: "To coin Money, regulate the Value thereof, and of foreign

Coin, and fix the Standard of Weights and Measures." Under a Constitutional money system, Congress has the power to turn precious metals into coins of an established, uniform weight and denomination. This was intended to be a protection against the debasement of coinage so prevalent throughout history.

Article I, Section 10 of the U.S. Constitution itemizes the few powers prohibited to the states, one of which deals with money: "No State shall...coin Money; emit Bills of Credit; make any Thing but gold and silver Coin a Tender in Payment of Debts." The states were not permitted to coin money, print paper money (bills of credit), or deem anything other than gold and silver coin as money. Paper money was considered a grave threat to liberty and banking institutions are historically the government's accomplices in producing it.

Any vagueness in the language of the Constitution on this issue is clarified when we heed the advice of the founders and simply resort "to the sense in which the Constitution was accepted and ratified by the nation, rather than try and squeeze some new meaning out of the text." It's clear from their own words that the framers of the Constitution would never have intended to give the federal government the power to debase the national currency through the printing press or any other means. Thomas Jefferson predicted, "If the American people ever allow private banks to control the issue of their currency, first by inflation then by deflation, the banks and the corporations that will grow up around them, will deprive the people of all property until their children wake up homeless on the continent their fathers conquered."

He also warned, "Banking institutions are more dangerous to our liberties than standing armies. Already they have raised up a monied aristocracy that has set the government at defiance. The issuing power (of money) should be taken away from the banks and restored to the people to whom it properly belongs." Jefferson, knowing the destructive nature of paper money, hoped that the American people would "crush in its birth the aristocracy of our monied corporations which dare already to challenge our government to a trial by strength, and bid defiance to the laws of our country."

James Madison concurred with Jefferson, and reminds us, "History records that the money changers have used every form of abuse, intrigue, deceit, and violent means possible to maintain their control over governments by controlling money and its issuance." Despite these strong warnings, our founders' fears were soon realized as the lure of paper money was a temptation too great to resist.

The Rise of the Federal Reserve

For one hundred and twenty-five years after the ratification of the Constitution, a struggle raged in the United States between those who wanted a centralized, national banking system and those who wanted a free-market, honest money system. The First Bank of the United States was established in 1791 and it immediately began issuing bank notes in excess of its precious metal reserves. The result was seventy-two percent inflation from 1791 to 1796. It's charter was not renewed in 1811, and the failed bank was shut down.

The lure of easy money and credit proved hard for Congress to resist, and just five years, later the Second Bank of the United States was established. The resulting series of economic booms and busts throughout the early nineteenth century led Presidential candidate Andrew Jackson to run his campaign on a platform of shutting down the central banks, and establishing a free-market money system[20]. Jackson said, "Mischief springs from the power which the moneyed interest derives from a paper currency which they are able to control, from the multitude of corporations with exclusive privileges...The bold effort the present (central) bank had made to control the government...are but premonitions of the fate that await the American people should they be deluded into a perpetuation of this institution or the establishment of another like it."

Concerning the character of central bankers, Jackson charged, "You are a den of vipers. I intend to rout you out and by the Eternal God I will rout you out. If the people only understood the rank injustice of our money and banking system, there would be a revolution before morning."

In 1828, Jackson put to rest the notion that Congress could delegate their authority to coin and regulate the value of currency to an outside organization when he said, "If Congress has the right under the Constitution to issue paper money, it was given them to use themselves, not to be delegated to individuals or corporations." Despite these warnings, the champions of central banking finally won in the beginning of the twentieth century. Congress passed the Federal Reserve Act, ensuring that private banking interests would eventually gain control of the nation's money supply.

The Federal Reserve System was hatched at a secret meeting of representatives from the world's most powerful private banking institutions at an upscale resort on Jekyll Island. It was textbook collusion, with one simple goal: to establish a private banking monopoly and eliminate competition through government legislation. The Federal Reserve Act itself was sponsored by Senator Nelson Aldrich, who was a close friend of J.P. Morgan, and the son-in-law of John D. Rockefeller. The bill was rammed through Congress during a poorly attended holiday session, and signed into law an hour later by the President in 1913.

The Mission of The Fed

Even though the shady events surrounding the creation of the Federal Reserve (the Fed) are well documented, it sounds like a far-fetched conspiracy theory. Let's imagine for a moment that it didn't happen that way. Let's remove from our thinking this conspiratorial sounding story of mustachioed bankers collaborating in smoke-filled rooms. Let's just evaluate the Fed objectively, based on its own public mission statement, as a legitimate organization whose sole purpose is protecting the well-being and prosperity of the United States, and the American people.

The following is a quote from "The Federal Reserve System: Its Purposes and Functions," a publication of the Fed itself: "The Federal Reserve System is the central bank of the United States. It was founded by Congress in

1913 to provide the nation with a safer, more flexible, and more stable monetary and financial system. Over the years, its role in banking and the economy has expanded."

This publication goes on to identify some of the duties of the Federal Reserve in this expanded role:

1) Conducting the nation's monetary policy by influencing the monetary and credit conditions in the economy in pursuit of maximum employment, stable prices, and moderate long-term interest rates.

2) Supervising and regulating banking institutions to ensure the safety and soundness of the nation's banking and financial system and to protect the credit rights of consumers.

3) Maintaining the stability of the financial system and containing systemic risk that may arise in financial markets[21].

Let's examine the record of the Federal Reserve. In the last ninety-six years of existence has the Fed faithfully carried out its mission and achieved its stated goals?

The Record of The Fed

The Fed didn't get off to a very good start. When the Federal Reserve Act was passed in 1913, the American people believed that the Fed would result in financial stability, so that panics like the ones in 1873, 1893, and 1907, could never happen again. However, just sixteen years after the Federal Reserve Act was passed, the stock market crashed and the United States entered the worst economic crisis in history. The Great Depression of 1929 was a crisis defined by massive unemployment, price instability, and systemic, institutional risk.

In 2002, former Fed Chairman Ben Bernanke acknowledged that the Federal Reserve played a role in producing the Great Depression during a speech he gave in honor of Milton Friedman's ninetieth birthday: "I would like to say to Milton...regarding the Great Depression, you're right. We did it. We're very sorry.[22]" This was refreshing to hear, since apologists for the Fed often shift the blame of the Great Depression elsewhere. However, rather than seeing this as a repudiation of central banking, and the fractional reserve system as a whole, supporters of the Federal Reserve insist that it was simply a matter of the Fed not doing enough to prevent the Depression.

Price Instability

Let's fast forward to our current economic climate now that the Federal Reserve has a few more decades of experience under its belt. How has the central bank contributed to price stability over the past eighty years? Here's what former Fed Chairman Alan Greenspan had to say about it in 2002: "It was the case that the price level in 1929 was not much different, on net, from what it had been in 1800...but in the two decades following 1933, the consumer price index in the United States nearly doubled. And, in the four decades after that, prices quintupled.[23]" Greenspan admits that price levels on the whole were stable for over one hundred years. Inflation was almost nonexistent prior to the Federal Reserve.

We tend to define inflation as rising prices. Rising prices are not inflation, but instead are the result of inflation. Inflation is the expansion of the money supply without a corresponding expansion of goods. When this happens, more dollars start chasing the same number of products. This results in the reduction of the purchasing power of the dollar, which is reflected in an increase in prices.

Once the power of the printing press was unleashed, and turbo charged with the power of fractional reserve banking, inflation spiraled out of control. The value of the dollar has eroded to the point that it now takes over twenty-two thousand dollars to buy the same amount of products that one thousand dollars could buy in 1913.

The Inflation Tax

Inflation is a nefarious, hidden tax. Even John Maynard Keynes, the father of modern macroeconomics, recognized the destructive nature of inflation when he said, "By a continuing process of inflation, governments can confiscate, secretly and unobserved, an important part of the wealth of their citizens. There is no subtler, no surer means of overturning the existing basis of society than to debauch the currency. The process engages all the hidden forces of economic law on the side of destruction, and does it in a manner which not one man in a million can diagnose."

Inflation is a transfer of wealth that benefits the first recipients of the newly printed dollars, and penalizes those who receive them last. As those dollars filter their way through the economy, the poor, the middle class, and the elderly are the real victims of inflation. By the time the money trickles down to them, prices have already increased.

In its mission of maintaining price stability, the Fed has utterly failed.

Economic Booms and Busts

The Federal Reserve also claims to protect us from monetary crises. However, The Fed is the source of the cheap money that fuels the economic booms that always go bust. Instead of being our protector, the Federal Reserve engages in exactly the practices which are guaranteed to result in crisis. Government established central banks artificially lower interest rates by increasing the supply of money through the banking system.

In 2003 to 2004, Alan Greenspan brought the federal funds rate down to one percent, and kept it there for a full a year[24]. More dollars were created under Greenspan than were created in the entire history of the United States. While this was supposed to "stimulate" the economy, what it really did was mislead investors, and fuel an investment boom that could not be sustained in the long run.

The Role of Savings

What many people simply don't understand is that sustainable economic growth and productivity depend upon an increase in real savings, not the artificial creation of wealth. When people save money, they trade present consumption for future consumption. In other words, people save money now to buy things later.

When people save money, banks must pay interest on savings. As savings levels increase, banks must lend more to generate interest revenue and give those people a return on their savings. To accomplish this, banks lower the interest rates on loans to encourage borrowing.

It's one thing when banks are lending at low rates due to an actual increase in the level of savings. This reflects an economic reality where money exists for future purchases, and encourages businesses to make long-term capital investments. Those expansions depend upon future consumption, made possible by higher levels of savings.

It's another thing entirely when the Federal Reserve arbitrarily adjusts interest rates regardless of savings levels, because it sends the wrong signal to the marketplace. The Fed's cheap money induces massive borrowing, moving scarce resources into risky ventures. Market signals of profit and loss are distorted, though a frenzy of activity gives the appearance of financial prosperity. In the end, financial reckoning day arrives, no matter what tricks the Fed uses to try and delay it.

The Housing Bubble

Consider the housing bubble. There is plenty of blame to go around for why the housing bubble occurred. Fannie Mae and Freddie Mac deserve some blame. These agencies guaranteed risky mortgages, and engaged in subprime lending. Their implicit guarantee from the federal government allowed them to take on more risk than was prudent, and encouraged similar risk taking from other banking institutions who wanted to remain competitive.

The Community Reinvestment Act deserves some blame. It subsidized risky lending practices, and encouraged the lowering of traditional credit underwriting standards to promote "home ownership." Banks who did not engage in risky lending opened themselves up to discrimination lawsuits, and could be barred from engaging in acquisitions and mergers by the federal government. Combine these factors with Wall Street's insatiable desire to package mortgage backed securities into sophisticated financial instruments, and we certainly had a recipe for disaster.

These factors alone cannot account for the stratospheric rise in housing prices. For sixty years, home values increased in tandem with the Consumer Price Index, at two to three percent per year. Then came the housing boom. From August 1998 to August 2006, median home prices increased by one hundred and fifty percent[25].

When the housing bubble popped, home prices went into reverse, falling by twenty-three percent over the next two years[26]. Foreclosures skyrocketed and have continued to mount ever since. Subdivisions and strip malls all across the country remain unfinished and unoccupied due to the unexpected crash of real estate values. In some parts of the country, home values have fallen by fifty percent from their highs. All the equity from the previous ten years has evaporated. Are we to believe that this is simply the result of predatory mortgage lending practices and Wall Street greed?

The financial fallout wasn't limited to the real estate sector. The stock market has followed a similar course. On October 9, 2007, the New York Stock Exchange closed with the DOW at 14,164.53, the highest close ever[27]. Thirteen months later, it closed at 7,552.29, a drop of over forty-six percent[28]. Even now, over two years later, the stock market is off by thirty percent from its 2007 high. Investment portfolios have been destroyed and may never fully recover.

The Federal Bartender

When businesses in every sector across the county, from construction, to retail, to education, experience a simultaneous recession, the simplest explanation is to look at what they all have in common: money. During the boom years, the Fed's manipulation of interest rates moved future purchases and investments into the present, creating a false prosperity bubble. These artificially low interest rates also encouraged speculation, in both real estate and the stock market, as investors sought higher returns in order to get ahead of anticipated inflation.

Everybody loves the boom years, and never wants them to end. In the same way that a night of binge drinking is followed by the inevitable hangover, God's laws of economics cannot be repealed. America was caught up in a frenzy of the fast buck. Home equity was used to buy Cadillac Escalades. Flipping houses was the sure way to quick cash. The stock market seemed like it would never hit the top. Now, after the crash, millions of people are out of work, losing their homes, and filing for bankruptcy. Many of these jobs are not coming back. The bubble is gone for good.

The misguided policies of Congress would never have caused such widespread damage without the Federal Reserve first providing the easy money. As Financial Advisor Peter Schiff points out, "Wall Street got drunk. Main Street got drunk. But who provided the alcohol?[29]" It was courtesy of The Federal Reserve Pub, with Greenspan and Bernanke as bartenders.

The record of the Federal Reserve is exactly the opposite of what the American people were promised when it was instituted in 1913. The Fed is the primary instigator of economic instability. Rather than stabilizing prices, moderating interest rates, and reducing unemployment, the Fed has institutionalized economic booms and busts.

In its mission of providing stability and protecting us from economic crises, the Fed has utterly failed.

Unsound Banking and Systemic Risk

What about the Fed's mission to maintain the integrity of banking practices to contain systemic risks? Has the Federal Reserve's supervision accomplished this goal?

In March 2007, former Treasury Secretary Henry Paulson told Americans that the global economy was "as strong as I've seen it in my business career." He added in March of 2008, "Our financial institutions are strong. Our investment banks are strong. Our banks are strong. They're going to be strong for many, many years.[30]"

Less than six months later, things had gotten so bad, Paulson virtually threatened Congress that without a seven hundred billion dollar appropriation, the whole financial system would collapse.

In October 2005, when Ben Bernanke was being considered for his first term as Fed Chairman, he claimed that there was no housing bubble getting ready to burst[31]. In May 2007, Bernanke said, "We do not expect significant spillovers from the subprime market to the rest of the economy or to the financial system.[32]"

Not only was the Fed unable to prevent the U.S. economy from coming to the brink of collapse, Bernanke had absolutely no idea that the economy was even in danger. In August 2008, our economy was in serious trouble. Paulson and Bernanke, along with the Congressional Budget Office, grossly underestimated the costs. They assured the country that, other than perhaps twenty-five billion dollars in bailout money for Fannie Mae and Freddie Mac, the fundamentals of the economy were sound[33]. To date, Fannie and Freddie have received five times that amount[34]. President Obama recently signed an executive order guaranteeing unlimited funds for these failed enterprises, all the way through 2012. This is a blank check to cover up to five trillion dollars in mortgage backed liabilities, courtesy of the American taxpayer[35].

Meanwhile, defenders of the central bank keep telling confused citizens that the central bank is not only essential to our economic survival, but is the only institution with the wisdom and experience to avert future calamity. Ironically, having set the stage for the current crisis, the Fed is sought out for the solution.

Many economists are praising the Fed for their swift action by which America has averted another Great Depression. These economists, who didn't see the crash coming in the first place, are working hard to assure us that America is now in the first stages of a recovery. Meanwhile, insolvent banks are being seized every week by the FDIC, unemployment benefits continue to be extended, and talk of another stimulus package echoes through the halls of Congress.

We Bought Into the Boom

As Christians in America, many of us were caught up with the rest of the nation in the Fed created prosperity illusion. We bought into the boom. Some even attributed this temporary prosperity to the blessing of God, focusing only on the short-term gains, but oblivious to the long-term pain. We built multimillion dollar church facilities, financed on variable rate mortgages. We based our budgets on the assumption that full employment, appreciating real estate prices, and bulging stock portfolios would go on forever. We spent the money during those years of plenty on ourselves, and failed to store up for the lean years ahead.

Proverbs 22:3 says, "A prudent man sees danger and takes refuge, but the simple keep going and suffer for it." The American church never saw this coming because we were ignorant about the nature of coin, currency, and credit.

As a result, church foreclosures and delinquencies are at a twenty-year high[36]. Instead of being positioned like Egypt under the wise leadership of Joseph, with a storehouse for the nations in times of want, what do we have to offer? In many ways, the church is in the same financial condition as the world. When we should be in a position to provide for both the spiritual and physical needs of the people in our communities, the American church is struggling to make ends meet.

Much of this can be attributed to our financial priorities being out of order. The largest evangelical denomination in America reported that for every dollar its churches spend on missions, five dollars are spent to pay the interest on the mortgage. For every dollar spent to meet the physical needs of people, eight dollars is spent on mortgage interest payments[37].

Without the generosity of the church, where do the people of this nation have to turn when they find themselves in the midst of a crisis? They turn to the government, who steps in to be the caretaker of the people. As a result, the church misses an opportunity to be the hands and feet of Christ.

80

The Coming Collapse

Some economists, who identify themselves with the Austrian School of Economics, believe it's far too soon to say that a second Great Depression has been averted. They are predicting a financial calamity of unprecedented levels if we continue on the course we're on. This coming collapse has been in the making for decades, fueled by the actions of the Fed.

Nowhere in scripture does God indicate that the Christians in America will not go through economic difficulty and hardship. Nationwide depression and hyperinflation may soon be a very real possibility, and Christians are completely unprepared to weather such a storm. The time may come when churches are the gathering places for people, pleading for help in time of need, begging for food and housing. Will the churches in America be ready to respond?

There is no way to build a financial hedge around ourselves big enough to avoid any potential catastrophe. No amount of preparation can shelter us from the hand of God should He choose to visit poverty upon us to accomplish His purposes. However, we would be wise to build our security on the wisdom of scripture, and have faith in the ways of God. Then, in the midst of such a crisis, Christians would be prepared to minister to the hungry and homeless instead of being forced to fend for our own survival.

The Federal Reserve has a government protected monopoly on printing money. The resulting inflation is theft, perpetrated by the Fed. The policies of the Fed produce debt-fueled booms that end up in depressions and busts. These busts result in unemployment, property loss, and despair. The tragedy is that all of this would be avoidable if our nation would return to Constitutional money. Our current Federal Reserve System, based on the fraudulent practices of fractional reserve banking, is incongruent with the Christian values of integrity and transparency.

As Christian Patriots, we should be on the front lines in America, demanding a return to sound money. It's time to rebuke our government and its accomplice, the Federal Reserve, for their role in destroying what was once the most prosperous and generous nation in the world.

Chapter Six:

Desire Peace with All Nations

"Peace, commerce, and honest friendship with all nations, entangling alliances with none."

-Thomas Jefferson

"If it is possible, so far as it depends on you, live peaceably with all men."

-Romans 12:18

Called to Avoid Conflict

Peace is not always possible. Conflict has existed between individuals since Cain murdered Abel, and nations have been fighting for nearly as long. At times, war cannot be avoided. This is a reality of the broken world we live in. Jesus says there will be wars and rumors of wars until the end of this present age, and Ecclesiastes 3:8 tells us that there is "a time of war, and a time of peace."

The New Testament doesn't mandate complete pacifism. Reasonable self-defense is within the scope of Christian liberty. The Bible tells us that at least two swords were among the disciples the night that Jesus was betrayed. When Peter cut off the soldier's ear, Jesus didn't rebuke him for being armed, but for using his sword at the wrong time. When it comes to handling conflict, Christians are encouraged to follow the example of Christ.

1 Peter 2:21-23 says, "For to this you have been called, because Christ also suffered for you, leaving you an example, that you should follow in his steps. He committed no sin; no guile was found on his lips. When he was reviled, he did not revile in return; when he suffered, he did not threaten; but he trusted to him who judges justly." Sinless and blameless, Jesus was the perfect man. He had every justification to fight back. Instead, He trusted God to carry out justice, and did not retaliate. Christian Patriots should always be the proponents of peaceful solutions and diplomacy before we resort to war.

Called to Love Our Enemies

Jesus commands us in Matthew 5:44, "Love your enemies and pray for those who persecute you." The way we love our enemies is by obeying Romans 12:17-21, "Do not repay anyone evil for evil...but overcome evil with good." 1 Peter 3 commands us to bless those who attack us, and Matthew 5:39 says, "Do not make use of force against an evil man; but to him who gives you a blow on the right side of your face let the left be turned."

Christians are called to trust in the Lord. Yet, when it comes to conflict resolution between nations, we are quick to adopt the world's solutions. Romans 12:19 commands us, "Beloved, never avenge yourselves, but leave room for the wrath of God; for it is written, 'Vengeance is mine, I will repay,' says the Lord."

There is a difference between self-defense and vengeance. Romans 12:21 says, "Do not be overcome by evil, but overcome evil with good." Revenge is rooted in the darkness of our sinful hearts. When we are attacked, our natural response is to strike back. Vengeance leads us to strike back irrationally, often demanding more than "an eye for an eye." If we give in to that temptation, God tells us that we are at risk of being overcome with evil. Does vengeance become moral when we do it as a nation? Can we condone actions collectively, done through government on our behalf, that we would never condone individually?

We have abandoned the counsel of God as a nation. As Christians, we have turned to the government as our protector and as our avenger. The power to declare wars, destroy nations, and send our young men and women into harm's way is a sacred trust with incredible consequences. What has our government done to earn that trust? Has our government been a faithful steward of finances, which is the biblical measure of trustworthiness? How often have our leaders failed to live up to our standards of morality and integrity? How often has our government failed to deliver on its promises to the American people?

Our founders encouraged us to have a great distrust of our elected officials when it comes to war powers and foreign entanglements. James Madison observed, "All men having power ought to be mistrusted." Thomas Jefferson reminds us, "Governments constantly choose between telling lies and fighting wars, with the end result always being the same. One will always lead to the other." Why should our government be any exception? Can we be sure that every war our nation engages in is just and worthy of our unflinching support?

Called to Disciple the Nations

In Matthew 28:19, Jesus commands us to "Go ye therefore and teach all nations, baptizing them in the name of the Father, the of the Son, and of the Holy Ghost." For almost two thousand years, the Christian church has existed in Iraq. It has survived the invasions of the Persians, the Muslims, the Mongols, and the Ottomans. It is estimated that almost one and one half million Christians were free to worship and build churches in Iraq under Saddam Hussein[38]. Only now does the church in Iraq risk extinction.

Saddam Hussein was a tyrant, but for Iraqi Christians he had one redeeming quality. He kept the radical Shiite militants from rising to power. The Shiites in Iraq were brutalized and oppressed under Saddam, while Christians were generally left alone. Since the U.S. occupation in Iraq began, the persecution of Christians has spiraled out of control as Islamic fundamentalists have risen to power.

The church in America has largely supported the war in Iraq. How many of us are aware of the plight of our Iraqi brothers and sisters in Christ? They have been the victims of church bombings, car bombings, kidnappings and murders[39]. The U.S. invasion of Iraq has turned hundreds of thousands of Christians into homeless refugees. Less than five hundred thousand Christians remain in Iraq[40]. It's more dangerous for Christians living in Iraq now than it was under the rule of Saddam Hussein[41].

The war in Iraq has also resulted in the deaths of hundred of thousands of Muslim civilians who had yet to respond to the Gospel[42]. These were men, women, and children with eternal souls, who wished no harm upon the United States. They were farmers, merchants, students, and stay-at-home mothers. They were people who did their best to exercise their natural rights of life, liberty, and the pursuit of happiness. They were souls for whom Jesus Christ came to Earth and died.

Does the American church grieve for them, or have we bought into the propaganda that every Iraqi is a potential suicide bomber? Christians who are so vocally pro-life when it comes to the murder of unborn children inside the womb, are silent about wars that claim the lives of children every day. Can we have a heart for discipling the nations when we desire to see them conquered in war?

Demand Constitutional Wars

We need to follow Christian ideals when we approach the issue of war. We should also heed the wisdom and experience of our Founding Fathers who were familiar first hand with the consequences of war and empire building. On the issue of war, just like every other issue, we must demand that the Constitution is obeyed.

James 4:1-2 tells us that the source of conflict in humanity is fleshly, not spiritual: "What is the cause of wars and fighting among you? Is it not in your desires which are at war in your bodies? You are burning with desire, and have not your desire, so you put men to death; you are full of envy, and you are not able to get your desire, so you are fighting and making war." This natural propensity toward conflict led the framers of the Constitution to be cautious about who was granted the power to declare war.

There have only been five Constitutionally declared wars in the history of the United States, the most recent being World War II. Since then, our military has seen battle across the globe in places such as Korea, Vietnam, Iraq, Afghanistan, Bosnia, Kosovo, Grenada, and El Salvador. Rather than through a declaration of war by Congress, these conflicts have been retroactively authorized after the fact, or authorized through a United Nations Security Council Resolution[43].

Congressman Ron Paul stressed the importance of a Constitutional declaration of war before entering Iraq in 2002:

> "A declaration of war limits the presidential powers, narrows the focus, and implies a precise end-point to the conflict. A declaration of war makes Congress assume the responsibilities directed by the Constitution for this very important decision, rather than assume that if the major decision is left to the President and a poor result occurs, it will be his fault, not that of Congress. Hiding behind the transfer of the war power to the executive through the War Powers Resolution of 1973 will hardly suffice."

The War Powers Resolution of 1973 was passed after the Vietnam War. It allows the President to commit armed forces to military action for up to sixty days without the authorization of Congress. This resolution established war making powers in the hands of the Executive Branch that would have astonished our founders. James Madison wrote to Thomas Jefferson, "The constitution supposes, what the History of all Governments demonstrates, that the Executive is the branch of power most interested in war, and most prone to it. It has accordingly with studied care vested the question of war in the Legislature."

Congress abandoned their Constitutional duties by transferring the power to make war to the Executive Branch. The founders were certain that if the Executive Branch was granted the power to declare war, it would increase the frequency of foreign entanglements. James Madison, who believed that war was at the root of big government, said, "War is in fact the true nurse of executive aggrandizement."

He also believed that the military apparatus resulting from perpetual war would pose an enormous threat to our freedom. He warned, "If Tyranny and Oppression come to this land, it will be in the guise of fighting a foreign enemy...The means of defense against foreign danger historically have become the instruments of tyranny at home...Of all the enemies of public liberty, war is perhaps the most to be dreaded, because it comprises and develops the germ of every other."

Our founders knew that governments have a tendency to exaggerate, or completely fabricate, the danger of a foreign threat in order to gain more control. Madison said, "It is a universal truth that the loss of liberty at home is to be charged to the provisions against danger, real or pretended, from abroad...No nation could preserve its freedom in the midst of continual warfare."

The Citizen Militia

Our founders believed that America needed to have a strong national defense. George Washington said, "If we desire to secure peace, one of the most powerful instruments of our rising prosperity, it must be known, that we are at all times ready for War." However, a readiness for defensive war against a foreign aggressor did not mean that the United States must have an enormous, full-time, military force at home and abroad. What we refer to as "national defense," the founders would have called "standing armies."

90

The United States currently has over seven hundred military bases in over one hundred and thirty nations[44]. Our military footprint is more vast than any other nation in history. Consider the following facts:

- •U.S. military spending accounts for forty-eight percent of the world's total military spending.

- •U.S. military spending is more than the next forty-six highest spending countries in the world combined.

- •U.S. military spending is 5.8 times more than China, 10.2 times more than Russia, and 98.6 times more than Iran.

- •U.S. military spending is almost fifty-five times the combined spending of Cuba, Iran, Libya, North Korea, Sudan and Syria, whose spending amounts to around thirteen billion dollars.

Depending on how the numbers are calculated, our total annual military expenditures are currently as high as one and one half trillion dollars every year[45]. This is not what our founders had in mind.

The Constitutional authority to raise armies and maintain the militia was never intended to be a full-time, professional military force on the government payroll in times of war and peace. Listen to how it's explained by Second Amendment scholar William Marina:

"The tradition of the citizen's militia was intimately related to the experiences of English libertarians in the English Revolution and the Glorious Revolution of 1688. The

Parliamentarians came to appreciate that the King, as the head of the state, could only be successfully opposed if his control of whatever standing army that existed for national defense was somehow weakened. This was done in two ways. The first was fiscal. Parliament had to gather each year to pass the Mutiny Act if there were to be funds for the army. It was because of this tradition that the Founders put into the Constitution that no appropriation for the army may be for a longer term than two years....The second way to cope with the peril to liberty of a standing army is to counter its existence with an armed citizen's militia which stands outside of the control of the government...Indeed, one of the important grievances that produced the Glorious Revolution had been the King's attempt to disarm the Protestants; the subsequent English Bill of Rights, forced on King William, had specifically guaranteed their right to arms...The defense of the realm was best entrusted to the armed body of the citizenry, rather than a standing army.[46]"

The founders believed that an armed population, outside of the control of the federal government, was both a superior form of national defense and the best means of protecting the people's liberties against the state's usurpation. The patriotic citizens of any free nation would never hesitate to take up arms and go to war in the legitimate service of their country. Both well-armed, and well-trained, these citizens would step up to the task. As one Whig pamphleteer put it at the end of the seventeenth century: "When the People are easy and satisfied, the whole Kingdom is the King's Army."

Are We Safe Yet?

We are living in the fulfillment of what President Eisenhower warned us about in his farewell speech regarding the military-industrial complex:

> "In the councils of government, we must guard against the acquisition of unwarranted influence, whether sought or unsought, by the military industrial complex. The potential for the disastrous rise of misplaced power exists and will persist...We must never let the weight of this combination endanger our liberties or democratic processes. We should take nothing for granted. Only an alert and knowledgeable citizenry can compel the proper meshing of the huge industrial and military machinery of defense with our peaceful methods and goals, so that security and liberty may prosper together."

After trillions of dollars spent, after decades of "spreading democracy" around the world, after deposing numerous tyrants all hysterically described as "the next Hitler," and after surrendering untold liberties here at home for the sake of keeping America safe, is it enough? It should be enough to convince any Christian Patriot that only God can truly protect America from danger, while every effort of government to eliminate evil from the globe will be in vain. Reducing federal spending on "national defense" is a politically incorrect suggestion on both sides of the partisan aisle. It can elicit accusations of trying to weaken America or deprive our soldiers of bullets and body armor.

Nation building and national defense are not the same thing. If it makes me unpatriotic to suggest that we must eliminate standing armies, stop policing the world, and cease wars of conquest and regime change, then I am in good company. Listen to the words of Thomas Jefferson on the issue:

> "Yet at the same time that as a nation we must always be ready to take up arms against an aggressive enemy, we are urged to be wary of. The spirit of this country is totally adverse to a large military force...We did not raise armies for glory or for conquest...Conquest is not in our principles. It is inconsistent with our government...If there is one principle more deeply rooted in the mind of every American, it is that we should have nothing to do with conquest....I hope our wisdom will grow with our power, and teach us, that the less we use our power the greater it will be."

Our founders advised against the United States being embroiled in the problems and politics of other countries. They were opposed to the idea of policing the world, and spreading democracy through military force. However, the founders were not isolationists. They believed that the United States should engage in peaceful commerce, diplomacy, and friendship with all nations of the world. Jefferson said, "It should be our endeavor to cultivate the peace and friendship of every nation...Our interest will be to throw open the doors of commerce, and to knock off all its shackles, giving perfect freedom to all persons for the vent to whatever they may choose to bring into our ports, and asking the same in theirs." Jefferson believed all

94

nations would seek to befriend us because of the incredible fruits of our freedom.

The words of scripture and the wisdom of the founders are clear: Christian Patriots should be the proponents of peace, not war. As individuals and as a nation, we should seek to live peaceably with all men, not searching the globe for "monsters" to destroy. When war cannot be avoided, it should be Constitutionally declared by Congress.

Fidelity to the Constitution will prevent American soldiers from being needlessly sent into harm's way. It will ensure that the United States only engages in necessary wars of defense, with a specific mission and tangible end. It will reduce the chances that we will be responsible for needlessly taking the lives of innocent civilians throughout the world. A humble foreign policy is consistent with the vision of our founders, and will ensure the future of our nation's safety and freedom.

Chapter Seven:

Disciple Others in Liberty

"If a nation expects to be ignorant and free, it expects what never was, and never will be."

-Thomas Jefferson

"And the things that thou hast heard of me among many witnesses, the same commit thou to faithful men, who shall be able to teach others also."

-2 Timothy 2:2

The Disciple of Christ

A disciple is a student, a follower, and an adherent to a certain way of life or philosophy. As a Christian Patriot, our primary calling is to be a faithful disciple of Jesus Christ. Following the teachings of Jesus and modeling the life of Christ is the path of true freedom. The Bible is more than a handbook of do's and don't. It's a roadmap to a life of blessing and liberty in this life and into eternity.

If we want to grow as a disciple of Jesus, there are three things we must do. First, if we are going to live the teachings of Christ, we have to learn the teachings of Christ. Second, we need to connect ourselves with the community of disciples in the local church. Third, we must take what we know and multiply ourselves by making disciples. This method of discipleship can be credited with spreading the Gospel and the New Testament church throughout the world.

The Disciple of Liberty

The call to become a disciple of liberty is a parallel path of discipleship. If we are going to lead, we have to make sure that what we believe rests firmly upon a solid foundation. In the same way the Apostle Paul admonished us to understand the doctrines of Christianity in order to contend for our faith, we must have a working knowledge of the heritage of freedom and liberty established at the founding of this nation.

First, we must learn the principles of liberty as espoused by our founders. To ensure that our doctrine is pure, it's best to go directly to the source. The Declaration of Independence, the U.S. Constitution, Thomas Paine's "Common Sense," and the Anti-Federalist Papers are a good place to begin.

We need to know what men like Thomas Jefferson, James Madison, and Patrick Henry really thought and believed. We need to glean the wisdom from men like Samuel Adams and George Washington, who risked their lives and laid their fortunes on the line. What was their vision of freedom for America?

Not only should we read the writings of the founders, but we should also consult our contemporary mentors of liberty such as Murray Rothbard, Harry Browne, Ron Paul, Ludwig Von Mises, Judge Andrew Napolitano, and countless others. These individuals have sought to carry the torch of freedom and pass it on to us. Over the past century, they have taken our founders' philosophy of freedom and put it into the context of the issues we face today.

The Community of Liberty

Second, we must connect with a local community of patriots. The Liberty Movement isn't all about politics, it's also about community. The community confirms that we are not alone in what we believe. Much like the local church, the liberty community is bound together by our shared, core doctrines.

Getting involved in a vibrant, local community is just as essential to our growth as a disciple of liberty as the local church is in our growth as a disciple of Christ. It's in local meetings, rallies, and demonstrations that we learn together and work together. Some people have been fighting to preserve liberty for decades, while others are brand new. The local liberty community is where we can begin to find mentors, and mentor others. It is also where we can begin to exercise our talents and abilities, and contribute our resources to make a real difference.

The Anatomy of a Revolution

Nobody is an army of one. We all have a part to play. Everyone has strengths and limitations. The sooner we manage to leverage our strengths, and compensate for our weaknesses, the faster we'll be effective. We need to know where we fit in to the grand scheme of things, and help others find their place as well. Effective grassroots organizations are full of people who know their strengths and limitations, and have leaders who know how to deploy them.

We might use the term "organization" to describe our local liberty group, but it's not really an organization. It's an organism: a living entity that moves, grows, and reproduces. 1 Corinthians 12:12-20 describes a healthy, local church as a body in which every member plays a vital role:

> "The body is a unit, though it is made up of many
> parts; and though all its parts are many, they form
> one body. So it is with Christ. For we were all

baptized by one Spirit into one body—whether Jews or Greeks, slave or free—and we were all given the one Spirit to drink. Now the body is not made up of one part but of many. If the foot should say, 'Because I am not a hand, I do not belong to the body,' it would not for that reason cease to be part of the body. And if the ear should say, 'Because I am not an eye, I do not belong to the body,' it would not for that reason cease to be part of the body. If the whole body were an eye, where would the sense of hearing be? If the whole body were an ear, where would the sense of smell be? But in fact God has arranged the parts in the body, every one of them, just as he wanted them to be. If they were all one part, where would the body be? As it is, there are many parts, but one body."

When it comes to the church, Jesus Christ is the head. He sets the direction, and the Body of Christ follows. In the liberty movement, there is no single leader calling the shots. Instead, it's the Constitution, and the underlying philosophy of liberty that operates as the brains. Each of us are the members in particular, and we all have a part to play. Some of the roles in the liberty community are:

The Mouth

The "mouths" are the passionate speakers and teachers. They thrive on opportunities to teach, motivate, and inspire others. You may be a "mouth" even if you hate getting up and speaking in front of people. Media relations and issuing press releases are vital forms of communication that occur over the phone or behind a laptop computer. The "mouths" carry the message out to the masses, and expand the movement through education.

The Eyes

The "eyes" have the vision for the next steps that need to be taken, and see where the community needs to go. They discern which issues to tackle, what events to participate in, and how everything fits into the big picture. "Eyes" are essential to identifying future obstacles and helping the community to avoid them. This includes recognizing and avoiding issues that might divide the group, dilute the message, and destroy the momentum. The "eyes" help to keep the whole body on course.

The Hands

Grassroots groups are severely handicapped without a good set of "hands." The "hands" are the administrators who handle critical behind the scenes work that ensures everything goes off without a hitch. These valuable individuals do much of the heavy lifting, but often go unthanked and unnoticed. If you are the kind of person who doesn't mind if someone else gets the credit for all of your hard work, you might be a "hand." "Hands" manage databases of information, secure permits for rallies, and make copies of DVD's and fliers.

The Feet

"Feet" are the boots on the ground of the grassroots infantry. They are the signature gatherers, the door-to-door knockers, and the poll workers. The work of the "feet" is often as thankless as the work of the "hands," but the "feet" are subject to an even more brutal beating. They carry the movement forward and the whole body depends on them to get to its destination.

There are numerous other vital organs of the liberty movement, each carrying out a specific function. There are graphic designers, web-developers, financial supporters, accountants, legal advisors, video producers, and many others who give of their time, talent, and treasure to strengthen the whole. Each one of these roles is indispensable to spreading the philosophy of liberty and the growth of the liberty movement.

The Evangelist of Liberty

After we become a disciple of liberty, and find our place in the movement, we must engage in the work of making disciples. In the body of the liberty community, we are all called to reproduce. Disciple-making begins with evangelism, the process of reaching out and influencing others to embrace the principles of liberty.

Tea Party Patriots used to be the silent minority. Now, we are still a minority, but we are no longer silent. Making disciples will grow our numbers. With numbers comes influence, and with influence comes change. The success of our movement depends upon growing our ranks and gaining critical mass.

Find a Field

So, how do we begin making disciples of liberty? First, identify our field. This is the sphere of influence consisting of our friends, neighbors, and coworkers who already liked and trusted us before we became "right-wing nut-jobs." Statistically, that circle includes around seventy to one hundred real life people that we brush shoulders with on a regular basis. When we add to that our virtual sphere of influence on Facebook and Twitter, there may be between three hundred and three thousand people we can evangelize on a daily basis with the philosophy of liberty.

Plant Seeds

Second, we must start planting seeds. The current political climate provides us with a unique opportunity. Politics, once regarded as a taboo topic alongside religion, is now the substance of water-cooler talk in the workplace, and neighborhood conversations on the front porch. Average Americans are waking up and starting to engage. People are looking for answers.

Conversations about health care reform and global warming don't have to be heated, dogmatic debates. The point is to influence others to take the next step toward liberty, not to win an argument. Proverbs 15:1 says, "A gentle answer turns away wrath, but a harsh word stirs up anger." Humility goes a long way when trying to influence others.

Jesus asked questions to get to the heart of what people believe. We need to do the same thing. Get people to articulate their positions on health care, the war, the deficit, and sound money. Don't assume that you know what their hot buttons are, or where they stand, just because you know they voted for Barack Obama. Get people to verbalize what they really believe, and then ask them why they believe it. On average, it takes seven interactions to exert an influence on another person. Employ subtle, yet strategic, steps. When it comes to the seeds of liberty, patient plowing and planting ensures a harvest.

Anticipate the Harvest

Finally, anticipate a harvest. Just as it is in the very nature of seeds to bring forth fruit, the philosophy of liberty is sown deep within the soul of man. The Second Greatest commandment is truly the foundation of the philosophy of freedom. Love your neighbor as yourself. Treat people the way you want to be treated. Most people already believe this, and the spirit of independence is still strong in America. The right to be left alone and to keep the fruits of their labor isn't something we have to sell people on.

It's only a matter of time before persistence pays off, and the dormant seeds of liberty within people will begin to sprout.

A Legacy of Liberty

People are hard-wired by God with a desire to make a difference in the world. The ultimate realization of that comes when we engage in God's work of living the Gospel, and influencing lives for eternity. That desire to do something significant should guide us in everything we choose to spend our time doing. Christians and Non-Christians alike are getting politically active now for the same reasons our founders did over two hundred and thirty years ago. It's not just for ourselves, but for our posterity.

It's about leaving a legacy. Leaving a legacy is what inspires a soccer mom to wave a Gadsden Flag on the White House lawn. More than just a desire to stop national healthcare reform, it's the belief that what we are doing matters, makes a difference, and can shape the course of history.

I wrote this book as an introduction to the philosophy of liberty from a Christian perspective. Out of dozens of issues I could have discussed, I chose seven key priorities. Using scripture, and the writings of the founders, my desire was to challenge you to examine your core beliefs, and adopt a more Constitutionally consistent worldview.

This book is also an explanation of why I believe that political activism is an appropriate dimension of our Christian lifestyle. Political involvement is not a substitute for the Christian mission of evangelism and discipleship. That will always be the central calling of our lives. My desire is to present political activism as a moral and civic responsibility for a Christian. It's the alternative to ambivalence and apathy.

I am just a common citizen who has spent the last three and one half years being discipled, and discipling others, on the principles of liberty. This book isn't God-inspired, and you are certainly free to disagree.

However, if you agree, then this book is meant to be a manifesto, and a call to action. The hour is too late for us to wait for a political "messiah" of liberty to give us orders, and take us into the promised land. Its time for the people to lead.

A common refrain from many people in the growing liberty movement is, "I've never done anything like this before." If that's you, you're not alone. Thousands of regular people, with no political experience, are attending protests and rallies for the first time in their lives. They are starting local gatherings, and they are reclaiming their voice as "we the people."

No matter who you are, and no matter when you got involved in this fight, remember this: You always have something to contribute. Ideas spread person to person. The torch is handed from the older to younger generation. As an advocate for liberty, whatever knowledge you possess is a stewardship.

Go ye therefore, Christian Patriot. We need you to teach our nation.

The Unanimous Declaration of the Thirteen United States of America

When, in the course of human events, it becomes necessary for one people to dissolve the political bands which have connected them with another, and to assume among the powers of the earth, the separate and equal station to which the laws of nature and of nature's God entitle them, a decent respect to the opinions of mankind requires that they should declare the causes which impel them to the separation.

We hold these truths to be self-evident, that all men are created equal, that they are endowed by their Creator with certain unalienable rights, that among these are life, liberty and the pursuit of happiness. That to secure these rights, governments are instituted among men, deriving their just powers from the consent of the governed. That whenever any form of government becomes destructive to these ends, it is the right of the people to alter or to abolish it, and to institute new government, laying its foundation on such principles and organizing its powers in such form, as to them shall seem most likely to effect their safety and happiness. Prudence, indeed, will dictate that governments long established should not be changed for light and transient causes; and accordingly all experience hath shown that mankind are more disposed to suffer, while evils are sufferable, than to right themselves by abolishing the forms to which they are accustomed. But when a long train of abuses and usurpations, pursuing invariably the same object evinces a design to reduce them under absolute despotism, it is their right, it is their duty, to throw off such government, and to provide new guards for their future security. --Such has been the patient sufferance of these colonies; and such is now the necessity which constrains them to alter their former systems of government. The history of the present King of Great Britain is a history of repeated injuries and usurpations, all having in direct object the establishment of an absolute tyranny over these states. To prove this, let facts be submitted to a candid world.

He has refused his assent to laws, the most wholesome and necessary for the public good.

He has forbidden his governors to pass laws of immediate and pressing importance, unless suspended in their operation till his assent should be obtained; and when so suspended, he has utterly neglected to attend to them.

He has refused to pass other laws for the accommodation of large districts of people, unless those people would relinquish the right of representation in the legislature, a right inestimable to them and formidable to tyrants only.

He has called together legislative bodies at places unusual, uncomfortable, and distant from the depository of their public records, for the sole purpose of fatiguing them into compliance with his measures.

He has dissolved representative houses repeatedly, for opposing with manly firmness his invasions on the rights of the people.

He has refused for a long time, after such dissolutions, to cause others to be elected; whereby the legislative powers, incapable of annihilation, have returned to the people at large for their exercise; the state remaining in the meantime exposed to all the dangers of invasion from without, and convulsions within.

He has endeavored to prevent the population of these states; for that purpose obstructing the laws for naturalization of foreigners; refusing to pass others to encourage their migration hither, and raising the conditions of new appropriations of lands.

He has obstructed the administration of justice, by refusing his assent to laws for establishing judiciary powers.

He has made judges dependent on his will alone, for the tenure of their offices, and the amount and payment of their salaries.

He has erected a multitude of new offices, and sent hither swarms of officers to harass our people, and eat out their substance.

He has kept among us, in times of peace, standing armies without the consent of our legislature.

He has affected to render the military independent of and superior to civil power.

He has combined with others to subject us to a jurisdiction foreign to our constitution, and unacknowledged by our laws; giving his assent to their acts of pretended legislation:

For quartering large bodies of armed troops among us:

For protecting them, by mock trial, from punishment for any murders which they should commit on the inhabitants of these states:

For cutting off our trade with all parts of the world:

For imposing taxes on us without our consent:

For depriving us in many cases, of the benefits of trial by jury:

For transporting us beyond seas to be tried for pretended offenses:

For abolishing the free system of English laws in a neighboring province, establishing therein an arbitrary government, and enlarging its boundaries so as to render it at once an example and fit instrument for introducing the same absolute rule in these colonies:

For taking away our charters, abolishing our most valuable laws, and altering fundamentally the forms of our governments:

For suspending our own legislatures, and declaring themselves invested with power to legislate for us in all cases whatsoever.

He has abdicated government here, by declaring us out of his protection and waging war against us.

112

He has plundered our seas, ravaged our coasts, burned our towns, and destroyed the lives of our people.

He is at this time transporting large armies of foreign mercenaries to complete the works of death, desolation and tyranny, already begun with circumstances of cruelty and perfidy scarcely paralleled in the most barbarous ages, and totally unworthy the head of a civilized nation.

He has constrained our fellow citizens taken captive on the high seas to bear arms against their country, to become the executioners of their friends and brethren, or to fall themselves by their hands.

He has excited domestic insurrections amongst us, and has endeavored to bring on the inhabitants of our frontiers, the merciless Indian savages, whose known rule of warfare, is undistinguished destruction of all ages, sexes and conditions.

In every stage of these oppressions we have petitioned for redress in the most humble terms: our repeated petitions have been answered only by repeated injury. A prince, whose character is thus marked by every act which may define a tyrant, is unfit to be the ruler of a free people.

Nor have we been wanting in attention to our British brethren. We have warned them from time to time of attempts by their legislature to extend an unwarrantable jurisdiction over us. We have reminded them of the circumstances of our emigration and settlement here. We have appealed to their native justice and magnanimity, and we have conjured them by the ties of our common kindred to disavow these usurpations, which, would inevitably interrupt our connections and correspondence.

They too have been deaf to the voice of justice and of consanguinity. We must, therefore, acquiesce in the necessity, which denounces our separation, and hold them, as we hold the rest of mankind, enemies in war, in peace friends.

We, therefore, the representatives of the United States of America, in General Congress, assembled, appealing to the Supreme Judge of the world for the rectitude of our intentions, do, in the name, and by the authority of the good people of these colonies, solemnly publish and declare, that these united colonies are, and of right ought to be free and independent states; that they are absolved from all allegiance to the British Crown, and that all political connection between them and the state of Great Britain, is and ought to be totally dissolved; and that as free and independent states, they have full power to levy war, conclude peace, contract alliances, establish commerce, and to do all other acts and things which independent states may of right do.

And for the support of this declaration, with a firm reliance on the protection of Divine Providence, we mutually pledge to each other our lives, our fortunes and our sacred honor.

New Hampshire:

Josiah Bartlett, William Whipple, Matthew Thornton

Massachusetts:

John Hancock, Samual Adams, John Adams,

Robert Treat Paine, Elbridge Gerry

Rhode Island:

Stephen Hopkins, William Ellery

Connecticut:

Roger Sherman, Samuel Huntington, William Williams,

Oliver Wolcott

New York:

William Floyd, Philip Livingston, Francis Lewis,

Lewis Morris

New Jersey:

Richard Stockton, John Witherspoon, Francis Hopkinson,

John Hart, Abraham Clark

Pennsylvania:

Robert Morris, Benjamin Rush, Benjamin Franklin,

John Morton, George Clymer, James Smith,

George Taylor, James Wilson, George Ross

Delaware:

Caesar Rodney, George Read, Thomas McKean

Maryland:

Samuel Chase, William Paca, Thomas Stone,

Charles Carroll of Carrollton

Virginia:

George Wythe, Richard Henry Lee, Thomas Jefferson, Benjamin Harrison, Thomas Nelson, Jr., Francis Lightfoot Lee, Carter Braxton

North Carolina:

William Hooper, Joseph Hewes, John Penn

South Carolina:

Edward Rutledge, Thomas Heyward, Jr., Thomas Lynch, Jr., Arthur Middleton

Georgia:

Button Gwinnett, Lyman Hall, George Walton

The Constitution
of the United States

We the People of the United States, in Order to form a more perfect Union, establish Justice, insure domestic Tranquility, provide for the common defence, promote the general Welfare, and secure the Blessings of Liberty to ourselves and our Posterity, do ordain and establish this Constitution for the United States of America.

Article I

Section 1. All legislative Powers herein granted shall be vested in a Congress of the United States, which shall consist of a Senate and House of Representatives.

Section 2. The House of Representatives shall be composed of Members chosen every second Year by the People of the several States, and the Electors in each State shall have the Qualifications requisite for Electors of the most numerous Branch of the State Legislature.

No Person shall be a Representative who shall not have attained to the age of twenty five Years, and been seven Years a Citizen of the United States, and who shall not, when elected, be an Inhabitant of that State in which he shall be chosen.

Representatives and direct Taxes shall be apportioned among the several States which may be included within this Union, according to their respective Numbers, which shall be determined by adding to the whole Number of free Persons, including those bound to Service for a Term of Years, and excluding Indians not taxed, three fifths of all other Persons. The actual Enumeration shall be made within three Years after the first Meeting of the Congress of the United States, and within every subsequent Term of ten Years, in such Manner as they shall by Law direct. The Number of Representatives shall not exceed one for every thirty Thousand, but each State shall have at Least one Representative; and until such enumeration shall be made, the State of New Hampshire shall be entitled to chuse three, Massachusetts eight, Rhode-Island and Providence Plantations one, Connecticut five, New-York six, New Jersey four, Pennsylvania eight, Delaware one, Maryland six, Virginia ten, North Carolina five, South Carolina five, and Georgia three.

When vacancies happen in the Representation from any State, the Executive Authority thereof shall issue Writs of Election to fill such Vacancies.

The House of Representatives shall chuse their Speaker and other Officers; and shall have the sole Power of Impeachment.

Section 3. The Senate of the United States shall be composed of two Senators from each State, chosen by the Legislature thereof, for six Years; and each Senator shall have one Vote.

118

Immediately after they shall be assembled in Consequence of the first Election, they shall be divided as equally as may be into three Classes. The Seats of the Senators of the first Class shall be vacated at the Expiration of the second Year, of the second Class at the Expiration of the fourth Year, and the third Class at the Expiration of the sixth Year, so that one third may be chosen every second Year; and if Vacancies happen by Resignation, or otherwise, during the Recess of the Legislature of any State, the Executive thereof may make temporary Appointments until the next Meeting of the Legislature, which shall then fill such Vacancies.

No Person shall be a Senator who shall not have attained to the Age of thirty Years, and been nine Years a Citizen of the United States and who shall not, when elected, be an Inhabitant of that State for which he shall be chosen.

The Vice President of the United States shall be President of the Senate, but shall have no Vote, unless they be equally divided.

The Senate shall chuse their other Officers, and also a President pro tempore, in the Absence of the Vice President, or when he shall exercise the Office of President of the United States.

The Senate shall have the sole Power to try all Impeachments. When sitting for that Purpose, they shall be on Oath or Affirmation. When the President of the United States is tried, the Chief Justice shall preside: And no Person shall be convicted without the Concurrence of two thirds of the Members present.

Judgment in Cases of Impeachment shall not extend further than to removal from Office, and disqualification to hold and enjoy any Office of Honor, Trust or Profit under the United States: but the Party convicted shall nevertheless be liable and subject to Indictment, Trial, Judgment and Punishment, according to Law.

Section 4. The Times, Places and Manner of holding Elections for Senators and Representatives, shall be prescribed in each State by the Legislature thereof; but the Congress may at any time by Law make or alter such Regulations, except as to the Places of chusing Senators.

The Congress shall assemble at least once in every Year, and such Meeting shall be on the first Monday in December, unless they shall by Law appoint a different Day.

Section 5. Each House shall be the Judge of the Elections, Returns and Qualifications of its own Members, and a Majority of each shall constitute a Quorum to do Business; but a smaller Number may adjourn from day to day, and may be authorized to compel the Attendance of absent Members, in such Manner, and under such Penalties as each House may provide.

Each House may determine the Rules of its Proceedings, punish its Members for disorderly Behaviour, and, with the Concurrence of two thirds, expel a Member.

Each House shall keep a Journal of its Proceedings, and from time to time publish the same, excepting such Parts as may in their Judgment require Secrecy; and the Yeas and Nays of the Members of either House on any question shall, at the Desire of one fifth of those Present, be entered on the Journal.

Neither House, during the Session of Congress, shall, without the Consent of the other, adjourn for more than three days, nor to any other Place than that in which the two Houses shall be sitting.

Section 6. The Senators and Representatives shall receive a Compensation for their Services, to be ascertained by Law, and paid out of the Treasury of the United States. They shall in all Cases, except Treason, Felony and Breach of the Peace, be privileged from Arrest during their Attendance at the Session of their respective Houses, and in going to and returning from the same; and for any Speech or Debate in either House, they shall not be questioned in any other Place.

No Senator or Representative shall, during the Time for which he was elected, be appointed to any civil Office under the Authority of the United States, which shall have been created, or the Emoluments whereof shall have been encreased during such time: and no Person holding any Office under the United States, shall be a Member of either House during his Continuance in Office.

Section 7. All Bills for raising Revenue shall originate in the House of Representatives; but the Senate may propose or concur with Amendments as on other Bills.

Every Bill which shall have passed the House of Representatives and the Senate, shall, before it become a Law, be presented to the President of the United States; if he approve he shall sign it, but if not he shall return it, with his Objections to that House in which it shall have originated, who shall enter the Objections at large on their Journal, and proceed to reconsider it. If after such Reconsideration two thirds of that House shall agree to pass the Bill, it shall be sent, together with the Objections, to the other House, by which it shall likewise be reconsidered, and if approved by two thirds of that House, it shall become a Law. But in all such Cases the Votes of both Houses shall be determined by Yeas and Nays, and the Names of the Persons voting for and against the Bill shall be entered on the Journal of each House respectively. If any Bill shall not be returned by the President within ten Days (Sundays excepted) after it shall have been presented to him, the Same shall be a Law, in like Manner as if he had signed it, unless the Congress by their Adjournment prevent its Return, in which Case it shall not be a Law.

Every Order, Resolution, or Vote to which the Concurrence of the Senate and House of Representatives may be necessary (except on a question of Adjournment) shall be presented to the President of the United States; and before the Same shall take Effect, shall be approved by him, or being disapproved by him, shall be repassed by two thirds of the Senate and House of Representatives, according to the Rules and Limitations prescribed in the Case of a Bill.

Section 8. The Congress shall have Power To lay and collect Taxes, Duties, Imposts and Excises, to pay the Debts and provide for the common Defence and general Welfare of the United States; but all Duties, Imposts and Excises shall be uniform throughout the United States;

To borrow Money on the credit of the United States;

To regulate Commerce with foreign Nations, and among the several States, and with the Indian Tribes;

To establish an uniform Rule of Naturalization, and uniform Laws on the subject of Bankruptcies throughout the United States;

To coin Money, regulate the Value thereof, and of foreign Coin, and fix the Standard of Weights and Measures;

To provide for the Punishment of counterfeiting the Securities and current Coin of the United States;

To establish Post Offices and post Roads;

To promote the Progress of Science and useful Arts, by securing for limited Times to Authors and Inventors the exclusive Right to their respective Writings and Discoveries;

To constitute Tribunals inferior to the supreme Court;

To define and punish Piracies and Felonies committed on the high Seas, and Offences against the Law of Nations;

To declare War, grant Letters of Marque and Reprisal, and make Rules concerning Captures on Land and Water;

To raise and support Armies, but no Appropriation of Money to that Use shall be for a longer Term than two Years;

To provide and maintain a Navy;

To make Rules for the Government and Regulation of the land and naval Forces;

To provide for calling forth the Militia to execute the Laws of the Union, suppress Insurrections and repel Invasions;

To provide for organizing, arming, and disciplining, the Militia, and for governing such Part of them as may be employed in the Service of the United States, reserving to the States respectively, the Appointment of the Officers, and the Authority of training the Militia according to the discipline prescribed by Congress;

To exercise exclusive Legislation in all Cases whatsoever, over such District (not exceeding ten Miles square) as may, by Cession of particular States, and the Acceptance of Congress, become the Seat of the Government of the United States, and to exercise like Authority over all Places purchased by the Consent of the Legislature of the State in which the Same shall be, for the Erection of Forts, Magazines, Arsenals, dock-Yards, and other needful Buildings;--And

To make all Laws which shall be necessary and proper for carrying into Execution the foregoing Powers, and all other Powers vested by this Constitution in the Government of the United States, or in any Department or Officer thereof.

Section 9. The Migration or Importation of such Persons as any of the States now existing shall think proper to admit, shall not be prohibited by the Congress prior to the Year one thousand eight hundred and eight, but a Tax or duty may be imposed on such Importation, not exceeding ten dollars for each Person.

The Privilege of the Writ of Habeas Corpus shall not be suspended, unless when in Cases of Rebellion or Invasion the public Safety may require it.

No Bill of Attainder or ex post facto Law shall be passed.

No Capitation, or other direct, Tax shall be laid, unless in Proportion to the Census or Enumeration herein before directed to be taken.

No Tax or Duty shall be laid on Articles exported from any State.

No Preference shall be given by any Regulation of Commerce or Revenue to the Ports of one State over those of another: nor shall Vessels bound to, or from, one State, be obliged to enter, clear or pay Duties in another.

No Money shall be drawn from the Treasury, but in Consequence of Appropriations made by Law; and a regular Statement and Account of Receipts and Expenditures of all public Money shall be published from time to time.

No Title of Nobility shall be granted by the United States: And no Person holding any Office of Profit or Trust under them, shall, without the Consent of the Congress, accept of any present, Emolument, Office, or Title, of any kind whatever, from any King, Prince, or foreign State.

Section 10. No State shall enter into any Treaty, Alliance, or Confederation; grant Letters of Marque and Reprisal; coin Money; emit Bills of Credit; make any Thing but gold and silver Coin a Tender in Payment of Debts; pass any Bill of Attainder, ex post facto Law, or Law impairing the Obligation of Contracts, or grant any Title of Nobility.

No State shall, without the Consent of the Congress, lay any Imposts or Duties on Imports or Exports, except what may be absolutely necessary for executing it's inspection Laws: and the net Produce of all Duties and Imposts, laid by any State on Imports or Exports, shall be for the Use of the Treasury of the United States; and all such Laws shall be subject to the Revision and Controul of the Congress.

No State shall, without the Consent of Congress, lay any Duty of Tonnage, keep Troops, or Ships of War in time of Peace, enter into any Agreement or Compact with another State, or with a foreign Power, or engage in War, unless actually invaded, or in such imminent Danger as will not admit of delay.

Article II

Section 1. The executive Power shall be vested in a President of the United States of America. He shall hold his Office during the Term of four Years, and, together with the Vice President, chosen for the same Term, be elected, as follows:

Each State shall appoint, in such Manner as the Legislature thereof may direct, a Number of Electors, equal to the whole Number of Senators and Representatives to which the State may be entitled in the Congress: but no Senator or Representative, or Person holding an Office of Trust or Profit under the United States, shall be appointed an Elector.

The Electors shall meet in their respective States, and vote by Ballot for two Persons, of whom one at least shall not be an Inhabitant of the same State with themselves. And they shall make a List of all the Persons voted for, and of the Number of Votes for each; which List they shall sign and certify, and transmit sealed to the Seat of the Government of the United States, directed to the President of the Senate. The President of the Senate shall, in the Presence of the Senate and House of Representatives, open all the Certificates, and the Votes shall then be counted. The Person having the greatest Number of Votes shall be the President, if such Number be a Majority of the whole Number of Electors appointed; and if there be more than one who have such Majority, and have an equal Number of Votes, then the House of Representatives shall immediately chuse by Ballot one of them for President; and if no Person have a Majority, then from the five highest on the List the said House shall in like Manner chuse the President. But in chusing the President, the Votes shall be taken by States, the Representation from each State having one Vote; A quorum for this Purpose shall consist of a Member or Members from two thirds of the States, and a Majority of all the States shall be necessary to a Choice. In every Case, after the Choice of the President, the Person having the greatest Number of Votes of the Electors shall be the Vice President. But if there should remain two or more who have equal Votes, the Senate shall chuse from them by Ballot the Vice President.

The Congress may determine the Time of chusing the Electors, and the Day on which they shall give their Votes; which Day shall be the same throughout the United States.

No Person except a natural born Citizen, or a Citizen of the United States, at the time of the Adoption of this Constitution, shall be eligible to the Office of President;

neither shall any Person be eligible to that Office who shall not have attained to the Age of thirty five Years, and been fourteen Years a Resident within the United States.

In Case of the Removal of the President from Office, or of his Death, Resignation, or Inability to discharge the Powers and Duties of the said Office, the Same shall devolve on the Vice President, and the Congress may by Law provide for the Case of Removal, Death, Resignation or Inability, both of the President and Vice President, declaring what Officer shall then act as President, and such Officer shall act accordingly, until the Disability be removed, or a President shall be elected.

The President shall, at stated Times, receive for his Services, a Compensation, which shall neither be encreased nor diminished during the Period for which he shall have been elected, and he shall not receive within that Period any other Emolument from the United States, or any of them.

Before he enter on the Execution of his Office, he shall take the following Oath or Affirmation:--"I do solemnly swear (or affirm) that I will faithfully execute the Office of President of the United States, and will to the best of my Ability, preserve, protect and defend the Constitution of the United States."

Section 2. The President shall be Commander in Chief of the Army and Navy of the United States, and of the Militia of the several States, when called into the actual Service of the United States; he may require the Opinion, in writing, of the principal Officer in each of the executive Departments, upon any Subject relating to the Duties of their respective Offices, and he shall have Power to grant

Reprieves and Pardons for Offences against the United States, except in Cases of Impeachment.

He shall have Power, by and with the Advice and Consent of the Senate, to make Treaties, provided two thirds of the Senators present concur; and he shall nominate, and by and with the Advice and Consent of the Senate, shall appoint Ambassadors, other public Ministers and Consuls, Judges of the supreme Court, and all other Officers of the United States, whose Appointments are not herein otherwise provided for, and which shall be established by Law: but the Congress may by Law vest the Appointment of such inferior Officers, as they think proper, in the President alone, in the Courts of Law, or in the Heads of Departments.

The President shall have Power to fill up all Vacancies that may happen during the Recess of the Senate, by granting Commissions which shall expire at the End of their next Session.

Section 3. He shall from time to time give to the Congress Information of the State of the Union, and recommend to their Consideration such Measures as he shall judge necessary and expedient; he may, on extraordinary Occasions, convene both Houses, or either of them, and in Case of Disagreement between them, with Respect to the Time of Adjournment, he may adjourn them to such Time as he shall think proper; he shall receive Ambassadors and other public Ministers; he shall take Care that the Laws be faithfully executed, and shall Commission all the Officers of the United States.

Section 4. The President, Vice President and all civil Officers of the United States, shall be removed from

Office on Impeachment for, and Conviction of, Treason, Bribery, or other high Crimes and Misdemeanors.

Article III

Section 1. The judicial Power of the United States, shall be vested in one supreme Court, and in such inferior Courts as the Congress may from time to time ordain and establish. The Judges, both of the supreme and inferior Courts, shall hold their Offices during good Behaviour, and shall, at stated Times, receive for their Services, a Compensation, which shall not be diminished during their Continuance in Office.

Section 2. The judicial Power shall extend to all Cases, in Law and Equity, arising under this Constitution, the Laws of the United States, and Treaties made, or which shall be made, under their Authority;--to all Cases affecting Ambassadors, other public Ministers and Consuls;--to all Cases of admiralty and maritime Jurisdiction;--to Controversies to which the United States shall be a Party;--to Controversies between two or more States;-- between a State and Citizens of another State;--between Citizens of different States;--between Citizens of the same State claiming Lands under Grants of different States, and between a State, or the Citizens thereof, and foreign States, Citizens or Subjects.

In all Cases affecting Ambassadors, other public Ministers and Consuls, and those in which a State shall be Party, the supreme Court shall have original Jurisdiction. In all the other Cases before mentioned, the supreme Court shall have appellate Jurisdiction, both as to Law and Fact, with such Exceptions, and under such Regulations as the Congress shall make.

The Trial of all Crimes, except in Cases of Impeachment, shall be by Jury; and such Trial shall be held in the State where the said Crimes shall have been committed; but when not committed within any State, the Trial shall be at such Place or Places as the Congress may by Law have directed.

Section 3. Treason against the United States, shall consist only in levying War against them, or in adhering to their Enemies, giving them Aid and Comfort. No Person shall be convicted of Treason unless on the Testimony of two Witnesses to the same overt Act, or on Confession in open Court.

The Congress shall have Power to declare the Punishment of Treason, but no Attainder of Treason shall work Corruption of Blood, or Forfeiture except during the Life of the Person attainted.

Article IV

Section 1. Full Faith and Credit shall be given in each State to the public Acts, Records, and judicial Proceedings of every other State. And the Congress may by general Laws prescribe the Manner in which such Acts, Records, and Proceedings shall be proved, and the Effect thereof.

Section 2. The Citizens of each State shall be entitled to all Privileges and Immunities of Citizens in the several States.

A Person charged in any State with Treason, Felony, or other Crime, who shall flee from Justice, and be found in another State, shall on Demand of the executive Authority of the State from which he fled, be delivered up, to be removed to the State having Jurisdiction of the Crime.

No Person held to Service or Labour in one State, under the Laws thereof, escaping into another, shall, in Consequence of any Law or Regulation therein, be discharged from such Service or Labour, but shall be delivered up on Claim of the Party to whom such Service or Labour may be due.

Section 3. New States may be admitted by the Congress into this Union; but no new States shall be formed or erected within the Jurisdiction of any other State; nor any State be formed by the Junction of two or more States, or Parts of States, without the Consent of the Legislatures of the States concerned as well as of the Congress.

The Congress shall have Power to dispose of and make all needful Rules and Regulations respecting the Territory or other Property belonging to the United States; and nothing in this Constitution shall be so construed as to Prejudice any Claims of the United States, or of any particular State.

Section 4. The United States shall guarantee to every State in this Union a Republican Form of Government, and shall protect each of them against Invasion; and on Application of the Legislature, or of the Executive (when the Legislature cannot be convened) against domestic Violence.

Article V

The Congress, whenever two thirds of both Houses shall deem it necessary, shall propose Amendments to this Constitution, or, on the Application of the Legislatures of two thirds of the several States, shall call a Convention for proposing Amendments, which, in either Case, shall be valid to all Intents and Purposes, as Part of this Constitution, when ratified by the Legislatures of three fourths of the several States, or by Conventions in three fourths thereof, as the one or the other Mode of Ratification may be proposed by the Congress; Provided that no Amendment which may be made prior to the Year One thousand eight hundred and eight shall in any Manner affect the first and fourth Clauses in the Ninth Section of the first Article; and that no State, without its Consent, shall be deprived of its equal Suffrage in the Senate.

Article VI

All Debts contracted and Engagements entered into, before the Adoption of this Constitution, shall be as valid against the United States under this Constitution, as under the Confederation.

This Constitution, and the Laws of the United States which shall be made in Pursuance thereof; and all Treaties made, or which shall be made, under the Authority of the United States, shall be the supreme Law of the Land; and the Judges in every State shall be bound thereby, any Thing in the Constitution or Laws of any State to the Contrary notwithstanding.

The Senators and Representatives before mentioned, and the Members of the several State Legislatures, and all executive and judicial Officers, both of the United States and of the several States, shall be bound by Oath or Affirmation, to support this Constitution; but no religious

Test shall ever be required as a Qualification to any Office or public Trust under the United States.

Article VII

The Ratification of the Conventions of nine States, shall be sufficient for the Establishment of this Constitution between the States so ratifying the Same.

Done in Convention by the Unanimous Consent of the States present the Seventeenth Day of September in the Year of our Lord one thousand seven hundred and eighty-seven and of the Independence of the United States of America the Twelfth.   In witness whereof We have hereunto subscribed our Names.

George Washington--

President and deputy from Virginia

New Hampshire:

John Langdon, Nicholas Gilman

Massachusetts:

Nathaniel Gorham, Rufus King

Connecticut:

William Samuel Johnson, Roger Sherman

New York:

Alexander Hamilton

New Jersey:

William Livingston, David Brearly, William Paterson,

Jonathan Dayton

Pennsylvania:

Benjamin Franklin, Thomas Mifflin, Robert Morris,

George Clymer, Thomas FitzSimons, Jared Ingersoll,

James Wilson, Gouverneur Morris

Delaware:

George Read, Gunning Bedford, Jr., John Dickinson,

Richard Bassett, Jacob Broom

Maryland:

James McHenry, Daniel of Saint Thomas Jenifer,

Daniel Carroll

Virginia:

John Blair, James Madison, Jr.

North Carolina:

William Blount, Richard Dobbs Spaight,

Hugh Williamson

South Carolina:

John Rutledge, Charles Cotesworth Pinckney,

Charles Pinckney, Pierce Butler

Georgia:

William Few, Abraham Baldwin

The Bill of Rights

Amendment I

Congress shall make no law respecting an establishment of religion, or prohibiting the free exercise thereof; or abridging the freedom of speech, or of the press; or the right of the people peaceably to assemble, and to petition the Government for a redress of grievances.

Amendment II

A well regulated Militia, being necessary to the security of a free State, the right of the people to keep and bear Arms, shall not be infringed.

Amendment III

No Soldier shall, in time of peace be quartered in any house, without the consent of the Owner, nor in time of war, but in a manner to be prescribed by law.

Amendment IV

The right of the people to be secure in their persons, houses, papers, and effects, against unreasonable searches and seizures, shall not be violated, and no Warrants shall issue, but upon probable cause, supported by Oath or affirmation, and particularly describing the place to be searched, and the persons or things to be seized.

Amendment V

No person shall be held to answer for a capital, or otherwise infamous crime, unless on a presentment or indictment of a Grand Jury, except in cases arising in the land or naval forces, or in the Militia, when in actual service in time of War or public danger; nor shall any person be subject for the same offence to be twice put in jeopardy of life or limb; nor shall be compelled in any criminal case to be a witness against himself, nor be deprived of life, liberty, or property, without due process of law; nor shall private property be taken for public use, without just compensation.

Amendment VI

In all criminal prosecutions, the accused shall enjoy the right to a speedy and public trial, by an impartial jury of the State and district wherein the crime shall have been committed, which district shall have been previously ascertained by law, and to be informed of the nature and cause of the accusation; to be confronted with the witnesses against him; to have compulsory process for obtaining witnesses in his favor, and to have the Assistance of Counsel for his defence.

Amendment VII

In Suits at common law, where the value in controversy shall exceed twenty dollars, the right of trial by jury shall be preserved, and no fact tried by a jury, shall be otherwise re-examined in any Court of the United States, than according to the rules of the common law.

Amendment VIII

Excessive bail shall not be required, nor excessive fines imposed, nor cruel and unusual punishments inflicted.

Amendment IX

The enumeration in the Constitution, of certain rights, shall not be construed to deny or disparage others retained by the people.

Amendment X

The powers not delegated to the United States by the Constitution, nor prohibited by it to the States, are reserved to the States respectively, or to the people.

Bibliography

Bastiat, Frederic. The Law. Auburn, Alabama: Ludwig von Mises Institute, 2007.

Goyette, Charles. The Dollar Meltdown: Surviving the Impending Currency Crisis with Gold, Oil, and Other Unconventional Investments. New York: Penguin Group, 2009.

Griffin, G. Edward. The Creature from Jekyll Island: A Second Look at the Federal Reserve. Westlake Village, California: American Media, 2002.

Napolitano, Andrew P. A Nation of Sheep. Nashville, Tennessee: Thomas Nelson, 2007.

North, Gary. Honest Money: Biblical Principles of Money and Banking. Arlington Heights, Illinois: Christian Liberty Press, 2004.

Paul, Ron. End the Fed. New York: Grand Central Publishing, 2009.

Paul, Ron. The Revolution: A Manifesto. New York: Grand Central Publishing, 2008.

Rothbard, Murray N. The Case Against the Fed. Auburn, Alabama: Ludwig von Mises Institute, 2007.

Woods, Thomas E. Meltdown: A Free-Market Look at Why the Stock Market Collapsed, the Economy Tanked, and Government Bailouts Will Make Things Worse. Washington, DC: Regnery Publishing, 2009.

Endnotes

[1] Andy Barr, "2008 turnout shatters all records" Nov. 2008. http://www.politico.com/news/stories/1108/15306.html

[2] Rasmussen Reports "Just 21% Favor GM Bailout Plan, 67% Oppose" May 2009. http://www.rasmussenreports.com/ public_content/business/auto_industry/may_2009/ just_21_favor_gm_bailout_plan_67_oppose

[3] Rasmussen Reports "Support for Stimulus Package Falls to 37%" Feb. 2009. http://www.rasmussenreports.com/ public_content/business/economic_stimulus_package/ february_2009/support_for_stimulus_package_falls_to_37

[4] According to Webster's 1828 English Dictionary: "In the United States, treason is confined to the actual levying of war against the United States, or in adhering to their enemies, giving them aid and comfort." Elected officials swear to defend the Constitution against all enemies foreign and domestic. In violating the Constitution, they become a domestic enemy of the United States. Sounds like treason to me.

[5] Andrew P. Napolitano, *A Nation of Sheep* (Nashville: Thomas Nelson, Inc., 2007), p. 67.

[6] Andrew P. Napolitano, *A Nation of Sheep* (Nashville: Thomas Nelson, Inc., 2007), p. 77.

[7] Supreme Court Chief Justice John Marshall, McCulloch v. Maryland, 17 U.S. 316

[8] Andrew P. Napolitano, *A Nation of Sheep* (Nashville: Thomas Nelson, Inc., 2007), p. 67.

[9] Jeff Mason, "Obama to raise 10-year deficit to $9 trillion" Aug. 2009. http://www.reuters.com/article/idUSTRE57K4XE20090821

[10] David Lightman, "Bush is biggest spender since LBJ" Oct. 2007. http://www.mcclatchydc.com/2007/10/24/20767/bush-is-the-biggest-spender-since.html

[11] "Debt to the Penny and Who Holds It," http://www.treasurydirect.gov/NP/BPDLogin?application=np

[12] Jonathan Weisman, "Debt Limit to Rise to $8.18 Trillion," Nov. 2004. http://www.washingtonpost.com/wp-dyn/articles/A60963-2004Nov18.html

[13] "U.S. Taxpayers on Hook for $5 Trillion of Fannie, Freddie Debt ... No Matter What Barney Frank Says," March 2010, http://finance.yahoo.com/tech-ticker/u.s.-taxpayers-on-hook-for-5-trillion-of-fannie-freddie-debt-...-no-matter-what-barney-frank-says-438124.html?tickers=FNM,FRE,XLF,AIG,C,FAZ,JPM

[14] "Of Debts and Deficits," http://www.infoplease.com/cig/economics/deficits-debt.html

[15] Charles Goyette, *The Dollar Meltdown: Surviving the Impending Currency Crisis with Gold, Oil, and Other Unconventional Investments* (New York: Penguin Group, 2009), p. 6-7.

[16] Sharyl Attkisson, "Bailout Worst Case Tally: $23.7 Trillion," July 2009, http://www.cbsnews.com/stories/2009/07/20/cbsnews_investigates/main5175781.shtml

[17] Paul R. LaMonica, "China still likes us ... for now," Sept. 2009, http://money.cnn.com/2009/09/16/markets/thebuzz/index.htm

[18] "America Celebrates Tax Freedom Day," http://www.taxfoundation.org/taxfreedomday/

[19] Robert Reich, "Fed in hot water over secret bailouts," Apr. 2010, http://www.csmonitor.com/Money/Robert-Reich-s-Blog/2010/0401/Fed-in-hot-water-over-secret-bailouts

[20] Murray Rothbard, *A History of Money and Banking in the United States: The Colonial Era to World War II* (Auburn, Alabama: Ludwig von Mises Institute, 2002) pg. 68-82

[21] "The Federal Reserve System: Purposes and Functions," pg. 10, http://www.federalreserve.gov/pf/pf.htm

[22] Ben S. Bernanke, "At the Conference to Honor Milton Friedman, University of Chicago," Nov. 2002, http://www.federalreserve.gov/BOARDDOCS/SPEECHES/2002/20021108/default.htm

[23] George F. Smith, "The Root of Financial Panics," Sept. 2007, http://www.strike-the-root.com/72/smith/smith2.html

[24] Charles Goyette, *The Dollar Meltdown: Surviving the Impending Currency Crisis with Gold, Oil, and Other Unconventional Investments* (New York: Penguin Group, 2009), p. 11.

[25] http://www.irrationalexuberance.com/

[26] Henry Blodget, "The Housing Chart That's Worth 1000 Words," Feb. 2009, http://www.businessinsider.com/the-housing-chart-thats-worth-1000-words-2009-2

[27] Dow Jones Industrial Average (DJIA) History Chart: October 1, 1928 Through March 6,2009" http://www.nyse.tv/djia-chart-history.htm

[28] "RAW DATA: Dow Jones Average by the Numbers," Nov. 2008, http://www.foxnews.com/story/0,2933,455605,00.html

[29] Peter Schiff, "Why the Meltdown Should Have Surprised No One'" Mar. 2009, http://mises.org/media/2998

[30] Thomas E. Woods, *Meltdown: A Free-Market Look at Why the Stock Market Collapsed, the Economy Tanked, and Government Bailouts Will Make Things Worse* (Washington D.C.: Regnery Publishing, 2009), p. 37.

[31] Nell Henderson, "Bernanke: There's No Housing Bubble to Go Bust," Oct. 2005, http://www.washingtonpost.com/wp-dyn/content/article/2005/10/26/AR2005102602255.html

[32] Ben S. Bernanke, "At the Federal Reserve Bank of Chicago's 43rd Annual Conference on Bank Structure and Competition," May, 2007, http://www.federalreserve.gov/newsevents/speech/bernanke20070517a.htm

[33] Jeanne Sahadi, "Cost of Fannie, Freddie rescue - $25B," Jul. 2008, http://money.cnn.com/2008/07/22/news/economy/cbo_gse_rescue_costestim/

[34] Ben Protess, "Why Fannie and Freddie Continue to Cost Taxpayers Billions," Mar. 2010, http://huffpostfund.org/stories/2010/03/why-fannie-and-freddie-continue-cost-taxpayers-billions

[35] James R. Hagerty and Jessica Holzer, "U.S. Move to Cover Fannie, Freddie Losses Stirs Controversy," Dec. 2009, http://online.wsj.com/article/SB126168307200704747.html

[36] Martha C. White, "Let us now pray: Church mortgage delinquencies on the rise," Nov. 2009, http://www.walletpop.com/blog/2009/11/23/let-us-now-pray-church-mortgage-delinquencies-on-the-rise/

[37] "Debt, Church and Christians," http://www.jesusdrivenlife.org/debt.htm

[38] Daniel Pipes, "Iraq's Disappearing Christians," Aug. 2004, http://www.christiansofiraq.com/diapearing.html

[39] Michael Ireland, "Iraq: Worse for Christians Now Than under Saddam Hussein," July 2008, http://www.freerepublic.com/focus/f-news/2043737/posts

[40] Ethan Cole, "Christian Student Killed in Iraq; Fourth Murder in Days," Feb. 2010, http://www.christianpost.com/article/20100218/christian-student-killed-in-iraq-fourth-murder-in-days/index.html

[41] Canon Andrew White, "Iraq: The most dangerous place in the world for Christians," Mar. 2009, http://blogs.telegraph.co.uk/news/canonandrewwhite/9307626/Iraq_The_most_dangerous_place_in_the_world_for_Christians/

[42] Stephen M. Walt, "Why they hate us (II): How many Muslims has the U.S. killed in the past 30 years?," Nov. 2009, http://walt.foreignpolicy.com/posts/2009/11/30/why_they_hate_us_ii_how_many_muslims_has_the_us_killed_in_the_past_30_years

[43] "Declaration of War by the United States," Apr. 2010, http://wapedia.mobi/en/Declaration_of_war_by_the_United_States

[44] Chalmers Johnson, "America's Empire of Bases," Jul. 2004, http://www.fff.org/freedom/fd0404e.asp

[45] Jason Ditz, "Price of US Wars: $1 Trillion and Rising" Jan. 2010, http://news.antiwar.com/2010/01/26/price-of-us-wars-1-trillion-and-rising/

[46] William Marina, "Militia, Standing Armies, and the Second Amendment," July 1975, http://www.independent.org/newsroom/article.asp?id=1495

145

About The Author

Jason Rink is the Co-Founder and Director of Education for the Ohio Freedom Alliance. He is a member of the Board of Directors of the Ohio Liberty Council. He has appeared as a guest on FOX Business Channel's "America's Nightly Scoreboard," the FOX News program "On The Record with Greta Van Susteren," and "Freedom Watch" with Judge Andrew Napolitano. He is a contributing author of "Ron Paul: A Life of Ideas," the biography of Congressman Ron Paul. His work has been featured on the Libertarian website Lewrockwell.com. He is also the publisher of the grassroots, independent news publication, "The Liberty Voice."

Jason is an ordained minister, and previously worked as a pastor at The Bridge, a non-denominational church in Cincinnati, Ohio.

He lives in Columbus, Ohio with his wife of eleven years, Tisa, his ten year old son, Ethan, and dog, Rocco.

If you are interested in having him speak at an event, please contact him via email.

Website: www.jasonrink.com

Email: me@jasonrink.com